30 Minute Vegetar

30 Minute Vegetarian
Turkish Cookbook

Sarah Beattie

Thorsons

For Richard Oakley, who would have enjoyed it

Thorsons
An imprint of HarperCollins*Publishers*
1 London Bridge Street
London SE1 9GF

www.harpercollins.co.uk

Published by Thorsons 1998

1

© Sarah Beattie 1998

Sarah Beattie asserts the moral right to be
identified as the author of this work

A catalogue record of this book is
available from the British Library

ISBN 978-0-7225-3624-7

Printed and bound by Clays Ltd, St Ives plc

MIX
Paper from
responsible sources
FSC® C007454

FSC is a non-profit international organisation established to promote
the responsible management of the world's forests. Products carrying
the FSC label are independently certified to assure consumers that they
come from forests that are managed to meet the social, economic
and ecological needs of present and future generations.

Find out more about HarperCollins and the environment at
www.harpercollins.co.uk/green

Contents

Thanks are due to: the gentlemen of the Pamukkale, Kamil Koç and Ulasoy bus companies who took us safely along hundreds of miles of some frankly terrifying roads; the Turkish restaurateurs and hoteliers, whose warmth and hospitality make any stay in Turkey a pleasure; the downtrodden but still lovely Turkish Railways, especially Adana's Stationmaster and his friend; Min Mennie, Dot Hall, Glen Goodman and Mick Dolan; the Marhaba delicatessen, Scarborough; Bess Coslett; Wendy Coslett, Donna Sclater and Polly Oakley for continuous moral support; Brian Hasnip; Tess Missen and her goats; Bill and his aubergines (egg-plants) and other veg; Wanda Whiteley, who was so convinced she went to see for herself; *The Rough Guide to Turkey* and *Cadogan Guide: Turkey*;

and most especially to:

Michael Gray, Dylan Beattie and Magdalena Gray whose assistance in tasting and testing is as always invaluable and without whose love and conviction this book would probably not have been written.

Introduction

Turkey is a vast country that covers many different climatic regions. The range of produce available is huge and the influences from Europe, Asia and the Middle East have combined in a glorious mix of styles and flavours.

Turkish food is one of the world's best kept secrets. In its extraordinary variety it has much to offer the vegetarian. The Turks, whilst not having any tradition of vegetarianism, have long enjoyed many dishes without meat. The chilled *meze* counters offer a feast of fresh salads, silky purées, unctuous olive oil–cooked vegetables, zippy yoghurt sauces, and much more.

The Turks claim to have been making both pasta and pizza (*pide*) for longer than the Italians. Pulses, rice, nuts, herbs and spices, integral to the vegetarian's larder, all play a major role in Turkish cuisine. There are many delicious egg dishes, including *Menemen* (a little like the French *piperade*) and çilbir (poached eggs in yoghurt, butter and paprika sauce). Fresh vegetables are used extensively. Light summery cold soups contrast with earthy lentil soups. Rich casseroles, delicate flavoursome salads, tempting pastries and creamy puddings are all part of Turkish cooking and can all be made within the allotted 30 minutes.

Some famous Turkish dishes have sadly not been included for time reasons – *Aşure*, also called Noah's pudding, takes several hours to prepare and contains some 40 ingredients to represent the 40 days on the ark. Some others, especially in the Cold Meze chapter, should, strictly speaking, be left to chill for some hours.

However, as they are also delicious hot, they have been given a place – preparation and cooking times are still under 30 minutes. These dishes are most useful to make the night before, leaving them in the refrigerator until you are ready to eat.

The recipes serve 4 people, except where otherwise stated. Authentically several dishes are served at each meal with bread, pide or pilav (a grain dish). Turks are very hospitable and sharing food is an important part of cultural life. Recipes are stuck to fairly rigidly – it is as if Atatürk's zeal for standardization spread from the language to the cookbook. A friend's Turkish neighbour was deeply shocked to hear that they had eaten fruit and fish together – this was just not done! If the changes for speed, modern kitchens and vegetarianism offend anyone, I apologize unreservedly. I have tried, in making these adjustments, to preserve the integrity of the dishes while bringing the enjoyment of them to a wider audience.

Stocking Up – Turkish Ingredients

Almost all of the ingredients in Turkish cooking are readily available in your local store. A few will need a trip to a specialist shop.

CHEESE

Turks use a lot of fresh white cheese – sometimes from goats and sometimes from sheep (although it must be said, travelling through Turkey it is often hard to tell which are which: the goats look sheepish and the sheep have goatees!). The cheese is not as salty as the universally available feta, which if rinsed can be substituted. I am fortunate enough to have a local source of excellent goat's cheese. Check out the delicatessen counter. Other cheeses include Kasar, similar to the Jewish Kashkavale or Cheddar; Dil, rather like mozzarella and Gökelek, for which you will need to use Parmesan or other grana.

YOGHURT

The best yoghurt to use for Turkish cooking is that sold as Greek-style. This won't please the Turks but we have yet to see Turkish-style reach the supermarket. It is thicker, creamier and less acidic than the bio and set types.

PASTRY

Frozen pastry is a boon to cooks in a hurry. Stock up with filo (it is the closest alternative to Turkish *yufka*), flaky and puff. If you can find it – try ethnic food shops – buy *kadayif* or *konafa* pastry (it looks like white vermicelli), it is simple to use and you will find both sweet and savoury recipes.

HERBS
The most commonly used herb in Turkish cooking is parsley. Try to find the flat-leafed 'Italian' parsley, it has a better flavour. When you find it, buy lots. It is used by the handful in many dishes. Freeze what you don't need straightaway and you can crumble it, from frozen, into dishes that you are cooking, saving time. Dill is also popular but is sometimes difficult to find – substitute fennel if unavailable. Mint is used in teas, salads and soups. These herbs are easy to grow either in the garden or on your windowsill.

SPICES
Buy small quantities of spices regularly and keep them in a cool, dark, dry place. Turks particularly use cinnamon, cumin, saffron, black pepper, chilli powder and sumac. Sumac might be difficult to find, it has a sour flavour and is sprinkled over salads. You can use a squeeze of lemon, if sumac is unavailable.

PULSES
Canned beans and lentils speed you on your way. Keep a good stock of chick peas (garbanzos), red kidney beans, white haricot beans and lentils in your cupboard. Of course, if you prefer, you can soak and cook from dried, except in the case of the red lentils, this will take far longer than 30 minutes.

NUTS AND SEEDS

Keep tightly closed packets of shelled walnuts, almonds, hazelnuts and pistachios to hand. Ground almonds and hazelnuts are good standbys as are black cumin, sesame, pumpkin and sunflower seeds.

RICE AND OTHER GRAINS

Turks use a long grain rice often with tiny pasta. Pilav and stuffings are also made from bulgar wheat and couscous, both of which are to be found in supermarkets and wholefood stores. Ground rice and semolina form the basis of many milky puddings.

FRUITS

Always keep lemons on hand. Melons, peaches, bananas, figs and apricots in season will make the perfect end to a Turkish feast. Currants, raisins, sultanas and dried apricots are used not only in puddings but pilav too.

VEGETABLES

Aubergines (eggplants) predominate – in the 16th Century there were already some 150 known recipes. New cultivars have meant that the tedious salting and rinsing is now a thing of the past. Buy glossy, unshrivelled specimens. Onions tend to be smaller and sweeter than ordinary cooking onions – use shallots or red onions as advised. The first Turkish cucumber I ate was a revelation – it had real flavour! The same is true of all salad crops and tomatoes – try to find the very best. Buy outdoor varieties whenever possible.

CANS AND BOTTLES

Canned tomatoes are always useful as is passata (Italian strained tomatoes). Turks enjoy pickles – red cabbage, baby aubergine (eggplant), beetroots (beets), peppers – and yoghurt balls in olive oil (sold as *labne*). These are a quick way of adding to your meze table as is a dish of olives, black or green. Bottled cherries and other fruits are good to keep in the cupboard.

OILS AND FATS

Best quality extra virgin olive oil is essential, use cheaper oils for deep frying. Butter is used extensively but in most – but not all – cases you can substitute vegetable margarine. A bottle of sesame oil will add variety.

SUGAR AND HONEY

If you are going to make many Turkish desserts you will need a lot of sugar! I have used maple syrup for speed in some cases. Keep flowery or forest runny honey for other puddings.

WINE

Although it has a mainly Muslim population, Turkey produces a lot of wine. In fact, they claim to have the oldest known vineyard, dating from 4000 BC. As the wines are not easily found outside Turkey, use a Provençal or similar red with many of the meze. *Şerefe* (Cheers).

Çorbası (Soups)

Cacık

Cacık is always described as a cucumber and yoghurt salad. I think it is more properly termed a cold soup. It is just perfect in the hot weather and makes a complete lunch with good bread and a fragrant tomato salad.

You need flavourful cucumbers, the best yoghurt you can find and make sure everything is really cold before you start.

3	large cucumbers, peeled and diced
	salt and pepper
750g/1lb 10oz/3 cups	yoghurt
125ml/4fl oz/½ cup	water
2 cloves	garlic, crushed
30g/1oz/½ cup	mint leaves
2 tbsp	chopped dill

	TO SERVE
12	ice cubes
a few	feathery sprigs of dill
1–2 tbsp	olive oil

1) Put the cucumber in a large chilled bowl and sprinkle generously with salt and pepper.
2) Whizz the yoghurt, water, garlic and herbs in a liquidizer until well blended. Pour over the cucumber and mix well. Leave in the refrigerator until ready to serve.
3) Place 3 ice cubes in each bowl. Ladle over the soup and top with a sprig of dill and a trickle of olive oil.

Domates Çorbası

A very simple tomato soup. Serve with plenty of crusty bread and squeaky fresh white cheese.

2 tbsp	butter or margarine
1	onion, chopped
225g/8oz/4 cups	spring greens, chopped (you can buy these ready-prepared in some supermarkets)
1 tbsp	plain flour
200ml/7fl oz/¾ cup	passata (Italian strained tomatoes)
1 litre/1¾ pints/4 cups	vegetable stock or water
	salt and pepper

1) Melt the butter and fry the onion until soft and golden. Add the greens and cook for 3 minutes, stirring frequently.
2) Add the flour and cook for a further minute, before gradually stirring in the passata (Italian strained tomatoes) and stock or water. Season well and simmer for 15 minutes. Serve.

Düğün Çorbası

This is Wedding Soup. Usually made with mutton, it is quite similar to the Greek Aveglemono, with the final addition of egg and lemon.

For this soup to work, it requires a really good stock – if you don't have any home-made, buy one of the fresh, chilled varieties now available. Stock cubes are not the answer here.

3 tbsp	butter
225g/8oz/2 cups	oyster (pleurot) and chestnut (brown cap) mushrooms, shredded
1 clove	garlic, crushed
1 tbsp	plain flour
1 litre/1¾ pints/4 cups	vegetable stock
	salt and pepper (optional)
2	egg yolks
	juice of a lemon
1 tsp	chilli powder

1) Melt the butter. Pour off 2 tablespoons and reserve in a warm place.
2) Fry the mushrooms and garlic quickly in the remaining butter. Stir in the flour. Cook for 1 minute. Gradually add the stock, seasoning if necessary. Simmer for 10 minutes.
3) Whisk the egg yolks and lemon juice together. Whilst whisking, ladle in 200ml/7fl oz/1 cup of the hot soup. Still stirring, add the egg mixture to the rest of the soup, to give a lovely unctuous texture. Remove from the heat.

4) Mix the chilli powder into the remaining butter and dribble over the soup. Serve.

Mercimek Çorbası I

This lentil soup is a comforting staple, even eaten for breakfast or late at night. Two versions are given, the second is lighter than the first.

1	onion, chopped
1	carrot, chopped
1 stick	celery, chopped
2	tomatoes, chopped
1	bay leaf
3	peppercorns, crushed
1 tbsp	olive oil
375g/13oz can	lentils
750ml/1 pint 7fl oz/3 cups	dark vegetable stock or water
	salt

1) Fry the onion, carrot, celery, tomatoes, bay leaf and peppercorns in the olive oil until colouring. Add the lentils and stock or water. Bring to the boil and simmer for 15 minutes.
2) Purée with a wand blender or pour into a liquidizer. Add salt to taste. Reheat and serve.

Mercimek Çorbası II

Try to find the pale orangey coloured lentils for this soup. If you have time to soak them beforehand, do. If not, measure out the lentils first and then cover with boiling water before doing anything else.

200g/7oz/1 cup	lentils (see above)
2 tbsp	butter or margarine
2	onions, chopped
1	bay leaf
1 tbsp	plain flour
1 litre/1¾ pints/4 cups	light vegetable stock or water
	salt
2 slices	day old bread, cubed
	olive oil
2	egg yolks
200ml/7fl oz/¾ cup	milk

1) Melt the butter and fry the onions until lightly golden. Stir in the flour. Cook for 2 minutes. Add the bay leaf, lentils and stock or water. Bring to the boil and simmer for 20 minutes.
2) While the soup is simmering, fry the bread cubes in the oil until golden. Reserve.
3) Purée the lentils with a wand blender or pour into a liquidizer. When smooth, add the egg yolk and milk and whizz again. Add salt to taste. Reheat gently and cook for 1 minute before serving with a scatter of the fried bread.

Pirinç Çorbası

This rice soup is so simple and fast – it can be even quicker if you use leftover rice and canned tomatoes. It makes a wonderful lunch with the addition of a tablespoon of Parmesan or a dollop of thick plain yoghurt and some good bread.

1 litre/1¾ pints/4 cups	water
75g/2½oz/a scant ⅓ cup	rice
350g/12oz/2 cups	tomatoes, chopped
1 tbsp	butter
	salt and pepper
a pinch	sugar
a bunch	parsley (chop the stalks and leaves separately)

1) Put everything except the chopped parsley leaves into a saucepan. Bring to the boil and simmer for 20 minutes.
2) Check seasoning. Serve with a sprinkle of parsley leaves.

Şafak Çorbası

The translation of this soup's name is Sunrise Soup – but I was unable to discover if this poetically describes the sky suffused with pinks and oranges in dawn's early light or the habit of many Turks to have soup, like porridge, first thing in the morning. You'll never go back to Cream of Tomato after this!

2 tbsp	butter or margarine
2 tbsp	plain flour
1 litre/1¾ pints/4 cups	passata (Italian strained tomatoes)
250ml/9fl oz/1 cup	water
	salt
250ml/9fl oz/1 cup	milk
4	egg yolks

1) Melt the butter and cook the flour in it until it begins to turn nutty brown. Remove from the heat and gradually add the passata (Italian strained tomatoes). A wand blender makes fast work of this. Stir in the water. Season to taste – watch out, sometimes passata (Italian strained tomatoes) has already been heavily salted.
2) Bring to the boil, stirring. Simmer for 15 minutes.
3) Using a whisk, beat together the milk and egg yolks. Whisk into the hot soup. Keep whisking over a low heat for 1 minute, then serve.

Tarhana Çorbası

Tarhana sounded so mysterious – I was told it took a day to make. You had to mix yeast, tomatoes, peppers, onions and yoghurt with flour and water and then you had to let it rise, knock it back, let it rise again and again until it rises no more. Then you have to pull bits off, put them to dry and then reduce the dried pieces to crumbs, pass the crumbs through a sieve and finally you were ready to make your soup! Slightly out of the scope of a 30 minute book – by a mere 1,110 minutes. BUT then I discovered that Tarhana is sold in Middle-Eastern shops and the soup can be made in just a quarter of an hour, so...

1	onion, quartered
125g/4oz/1 cup	mushrooms
1 clove	garlic
2 tbsp	olive oil
1 tbsp	tomato purée (paste)
1 litre/1¾ pints/4 cups	stock
90g/3oz/⅓ cup	Tarhana flour (see above)
	salt and pepper

1) Chop the onion, mushrooms and garlic in a food processor with the oil. Use the pulse button to get a coarse minced texture. Scrape into a pan and cook while stirring until the mixture begins to brown. Add the tomato purée (paste).
2) Mix a quarter of the stock with the Tarhana flour. Add the rest to the pan and bring to the boil. Stir in the Tarhana liquid and

cook for 10 minutes, stirring often. Season and serve with toast fingers or croutons.

Cook's Note

If you can't find Tarhana, don't despair, try Yayla Çorbası (see page 12) instead.

Yayla Çorbası

This is another rice soup, this time made with yoghurt. The buttered mint garnish is so lovely – try it with other soups too (it is wonderful in fresh pea and lettuce, but that's another book!).

If you haven't any leftover rice, use precooked (easy-cook) and simmer the stock for 5 minutes before adding the yoghurt.

1	egg yolk
1 tbsp	plain flour
125ml/5fl oz/½ cup	water
100ml/4 oz/½ cup	yoghurt
4 tbsp	cooked rice
1 litre/1¾ pints/4 cups	dark vegetable stock
	salt and pepper
1 tbsp	melted butter
15g/½oz/1 cup	mint leaves

1) Whizz together the egg yolk, flour, water and yoghurt in a blender.
2) Bring the rice and stock to the boil. Stir in the yoghurt mixture. Season well. Simmer for 10 minutes.
3) Meanwhile, warm the butter, shred the mint and combine. Strain the soup into a tureen. Pour on the minted butter and serve.

Cold Meze

Barbunia Pilaki

The Turks appear to have the same word for Red Mullet as red beans – this can be confusing for the vegetarian at large! No such problems here, of course this is a bean salad. Pilaki means it is marinated and so, although it doesn't take long to make, it will benefit from standing in the refrigerator for a while, if possible. However it is also very good hot, over rice.

90ml/3fl oz/¹/₃ cup	oil
1	red onion, chopped
1	large carrot, diced
1	waxy potato, diced
500ml/18fl oz/2 cups	passata (Italian strained tomatoes)
2 cloves	garlic, crushed
400g/14oz can	red kidney beans, rinsed and drained
1 tbsp	sugar
a good pinch	salt
2	lemons, 1 quartered and 1 squeezed

1) Heat the oil in a pan and cook the onion, carrot and potato until softening. Add the passata (Italian strained tomatoes), garlic, beans, sugar and salt. Simmer for 15 minutes.
2) Place in a dish. Top with the quartered lemon and dribble over the lemon juice. Leave until required.

Biberli Peynir Ezmesi

This is a bit like a potted cheese. Serve it with bread or cold toast
fingers or use as part of a meze spread.

1–2 cloves	garlic, quartered
200g/7oz/1 cup	sheep's cheese, roughly broken up
150g/5oz/²⁄₃ cup	thick yoghurt
1 tsp	chilli powder – add more if you like things hot, less if you don't
	extra virgin olive oil

1) Put the garlic and cheese in a food processor and, using the
   pulse button, chop them finely.
2) Add the yoghurt and chilli powder and purée.
3) Scrape into a deep dish, levelling the top. Pour over a little
   olive oil to cover the surface. Chill well until needed.

Çoban Salatası

Otherwise known as a Shepherd's salad. Freshness and quality of the ingredients is all.

Turkish green peppers are shaped like chilli peppers (long, small, thin-skinned) but completely mild. Use them if you can find some but if not you will have to substitute an ordinary small green (bell) pepper.

1	small mild onion or shallot, halved and thinly sliced
3	Turkish green peppers (see above)
2	large tomatoes, chopped
1	large cucumber, peeled and diced
2 tbsp	roughly chopped parsley
1 tbsp	chopped mint
	juice of a lemon
2 tbsp	extra virgin olive oil
	salt and pepper

1) Place all the salad ingredients in a bowl and mix them together with your hands.
2) Just before serving combine the lemon juice, olive oil, a good pinch of salt and a generous grinding of black pepper in a screw topped jar. Shake well. Pour over the salad and toss lightly. Serve.

Çingene Salatası

This is another simple salad that relies on really fresh ingredients. In the absence of the long, thin, dark green but mild peppers so commonly found in Turkey, use either Hungarian Wax peppers or a green (bell) pepper, cubed.

200g/7oz/1 cup white sheep's cheese, diced
4 tomatoes, diced
2 long green peppers, sliced into rings (see above)
2 tbsp chopped mint
olive oil (optional)

1) Mix everything together. Drizzle over a little olive oil if desired but this is not always done. This salad can be served with a dish of black olives and some lemon wedges.

Ezme Acili

This is almost the Turkish equivalent of a fiery Mexican salsa. I have used it in similar ways. It is very fresh tasting and wakes up creamy or eggy dishes and cuts the oiliness of others. It is also great with any fritters.

1	mild onion, quartered
1	large chilli, deseeded
2	large tomatoes, quartered
30g/1 oz/2 cups	mint
1 clove	garlic, quartered
a good pinch	salt
a good pinch	sugar

1) Chop everything together in a food processor. Use the pulse button, do not purée but reduce everything to fine pieces. Scrape into a bowl and refrigerate until needed.

Fasülye Piyazı

This is another bean salad, also marinated but it requires no cooking.

400g/14oz can	haricot beans, rinsed and drained
90ml/3fl oz/⅓ cup	white wine vinegar
2	shallots, halved and thinly sliced
2 tbsp	chopped parsley
2	long, thin green peppers, sliced
	or
1	small (bell) pepper, diced
2	tomatoes, chopped
4 tbsp	olive oil
2 tbsp	lemon juice
	salt and pepper
2	hard-boiled eggs, peeled and quartered
90g/3oz/½ cup	black olives

1) Pour the vinegar over the beans and mix in the shallots and parsley. Leave to stand as long as possible.
2) Scatter the peppers and tomatoes over the beans. Mix together the oil, lemon and seasoning. Dribble over the salad and top with the hard-boiled eggs and olives.

Gökelek Peynir Salatası

Gökelek cheese is hard, dry and crumbly – much like Parmesan which you will almost certainly need to use in its place. This salad is quite strongly flavoured, serve it with some blander meze to balance things out.

1	large red onion, finely diced
4	large tomatoes, diced
1	small green (bell) pepper, diced
1	small red (bell) pepper, diced
2 tbsp	chopped parsley
90g/3oz/1½ cups	Gökelek or Parmesan cheese, freshly grated

1) Simply mix everything together in a large bowl and leave in the refrigerator until needed.

Havuç Tarama

Another yoghurt-based salad, this time with carrots. Some cooks parboil the carrots before grating, it gives a more velvety texture. Use this recipe also for grated celeriac (Kereviz) a sort of Turkish version of Celeriac Remoulade.

200g/7oz/1 cup	yoghurt
2 cloves	garlic, crushed
a pinch	salt
350g/12oz/2 cups	carrots, finely grated
2 tbsp	finely chopped dill

1) Combine all ingredients well. Chill until needed.

Haydarı

Yet another yoghurt salad, but this time it is very thick. It doesn't take any time to make but it does need time to drip. This stage can be cut out if you can find a very thick, drained yoghurt. However, the sitting time also allows the flavours to develop. Act according to time allotted.

30g/1oz/2 cups	mint leaves, roughly torn
5 cloves	garlic, peeled and quartered
450g/1lb/2 cups	yoghurt
	salt and pepper
½ tsp	sumac powder (optional)

1) Chop the mint and garlic in a food processor, using the pulse button.
2) Add the yoghurt, salt and pepper and whizz until well blended. Scrape into a sieve double-lined with cheesecloth and leave in a cool place until needed.
3) Sprinkle with sumac, if using, before serving.

Humus I

Virtually every chill counter of cold meze has one dish of Humus, sometimes there are two or three of slightly differing textures and flavours. Humus is popular all over the Eastern Mediterranean and now much of the world. Supermarkets sell it prepacked and on the deli counter but it is rarely as good as you can make at home. A food processor is ideal for giving you ultra smooth, creamy humus but judicious use of the pulse button can give you a coarser texture if you prefer.

420g/14oz can	chick peas (garbanzos), lightly drained
2 tbsp	tahini (sesame paste)
1 clove	garlic, quartered
2 tbsp	chopped parsley

1) Whizz everything in the food processor until smooth. Scrape into a dish and serve.

Humus II

This humus is lighter, less rich. I particularly like it with Manca (see page 31).

420g/14½oz can	chick peas (garbanzos), drained
2 tbsp	sesame oil
	juice of 2 lemons
1 tbsp	olive oil
1 tsp	chilli powder
6	black olives
a small bunch	parsley

1) Whizz the chick peas (garbanzos), sesame oil and lemon juice together until smooth.
2) Scrape into a dish. Combine the olive oil and chilli powder and dribble over the surface. Dot with olives and sprigs of parsley. Serve.

Imam Bayıldı

This recipe's name means 'the priest fainted'. There are supposedly several reasons for his collapse: from pleasure, from the amount of olive oil required, from overindulgence – take your pick! You need bread to mop up some of that oil. I recycle some of it by draining the aubergines (eggplants) and using the cooking liquid to stew garden peas and tiny onions.

Turks only eat this dish cold but you needn't.

	olive oil
4	aubergines (eggplants) – about 12.5cm/ 5 inches long
2	onions, thinly sliced
2	tomatoes, chopped
4 cloves	garlic, chopped
3 tbsp	chopped parsley
1 tsp	sugar
	salt and pepper
	water

1) Pour enough olive oil in a roasting tin to cover the base. Lay in the aubergines (eggplants), turning about to coat them, and bake at 230°C/450°F/Gas Mark 8 for 10 minutes.
2) Meanwhile, fry the onion gently. When soft, add the tomatoes, garlic, parsley, sugar, salt and pepper.
3) Slit the aubergines (eggplants) lengthways. Pile on the onion mixture. Return to the roasting tin.

4) Mix together another 4 tablespoons of olive oil with 250ml/9fl oz/1 cup of water and pour over the aubergines (eggplants). Cover tightly and return to the oven for another 15 minutes. Serve or cool and chill.

Ispanakli Salatası

This spinach salad is best made with whole baby leaves, but you can also make it with chard (then it becomes Pazı Salatası). The chard will need cooking in boiling water for 2 minutes before rinsing and cutting into strips. Ruby chard makes a particularly pretty salad.

450g/1lb/8 cups	ready-washed spinach
90ml/3fl oz/⅓ cup	olive oil
	juice of a lemon
	salt

1) Put the spinach in a steamer for 1 minute (half a minute if you have the baby leaves). Place in iced water. Drain thoroughly.
2) Put in a salad bowl. Add the oil and lemon juice. Sprinkle liberally with salt and toss. Serve.

Karnıbahar Salatası

Although this is a cauliflower salad, it works equally well (if not better) with broccoli. Turks seem to cook the cauliflower until quite tender – I prefer it with a little bite left. To leave it seriously *al dente* would be to change the nature of the salad but it is a question of personal taste.

1	medium cauliflower, broken into florets
2 cloves	garlic
5 tsp	salt
2 tbsp	extra virgin olive oil
	juice of 1 lemon
	black pepper
2 tbsp	chopped parsley

1) Boil or steam (or even microwave) the cauliflower until barely tender (or see above).
2) Meanwhile, crush the garlic with the salt. Mix in the oil and lemon juice.
3) Drain the cauliflower, refresh in cold water and drain again, thoroughly. Pour over the garlicky oil and sprinkle with freshly ground black pepper and the parsley. Serve or chill until required.

Kizilcik

Even aubergine (eggplant) haters seem to love this dish. You might have to double the quantities to cope with the demand but that's OK, it couldn't be much simpler to make.

1	large aubergine (eggplant)
	olive oil
4 tbsp	plain yoghurt
1–2 cloves	garlic, crushed
pinch	paprika
	or
	chopped parsley (optional)

1) Cut the aubergine (eggplant) into 1cm/½ inch cubes. Spread out in a roasting tin. Drizzle with olive oil.

2) Place in the hottest oven you can get at 240°C/475°F/Gas Mark 9 for 10 minutes, shaking the tin from time to time. The cubes will be nicely roasted. Place in a flat dish.

3) Mix together the yoghurt and garlic. When the aubergine (eggplant) has cooled a little, spread over the yoghurt. Dust with paprika or sprinkle with parsley, if liked. Leave in the fridge until serving.

Köy Salatası

I have never understood why this salad, the 'Village' salad contains sheep's cheese when the Shepherd's Salad (see page 16) doesn't. Very odd! This is very close to the archetypal Greek Salad.

1	cos (romaine) lettuce, washed and shredded
a small bunch	spring onions (scallions), chopped
2	medium tomatoes, diced
125g/4oz/1 cup	white sheep's cheese, diced
2 tbsp	chopped parsley
6	mint leaves, shredded
2 tbsp	extra virgin olive oil
1	lemon, quartered
12	black olives

1) Line 4 small plates with the lettuce. Scatter over the spring onions (scallions). Top with the tomatoes. Strew with the cheese. Sprinkle with the herbs. Drizzle with the oil and top with the lemon quarters and the olives. Serve. (Each diner adds as much lemon as desired.)

Manca

Traditionally, this is a fried dish which is served cold. It is easier to prepare all the vegetables and then roast them in a hot oven for 10 minutes. If you want them cold quickly, leave the cooked vegetables to stand 10 minutes, then simply fill the sink with ice cubes and stand the roasting tin on top.

1	large aubergine (eggplant)
	or
2	small aubergines (eggplants), diced
4	long green peppers, sliced
	or
2	green (bell) peppers, diced
3 cloves	garlic, thinly sliced
3	slightly under-ripe tomatoes, cubed
	olive oil

1) Mix all the vegetables together in a roasting tin.
2) Drizzle over the oil and bake at 230°C/450°F/Gas Mark 8 for 10 minutes, shaking the tin occasionally.
3) Cool and serve.

Pancar Salatası

This is a shocking pink salad, the colour is quite arresting. Use ready cooked vacuum-packed beetroots (beets) – not the pickled sort, as the vinegar used is often very harsh.

4	medium beetroots (beets) (see above)
a good pinch	sugar
1 tbsp	vinegar
200g/7oz/1 cup	plain yoghurt
2–3 cloves	garlic, crushed
	salt

1) Grate the beetroot (beets) – use a food processor for speed and to avoid staining your hands.
2) Put the beetroot (beets) in a bowl. Sprinkle over the sugar and vinegar.
3) Combine the yoghurt, garlic and a good pinch of salt. Pour over the beetroots (beets) and carefully mix well with a fork. Leave in the refrigerator until ready to serve.

Patates Salatası I

The cold meze cabinet contains at least one potato salad. Sometimes it is the more familiar mayonnaise-coated potato cubes but more usually it is something lighter. This is the simplest; essentially it is a potato vinaigrette. The second has other ingredients. Choose small waxy potatoes such as Charlotte and Ratte.

450g/1lb/2½ cups	small potatoes
3 tbsp	extra virgin olive oil
	juice of 1 lemon
3 tbsp	chopped parsley
	salt and pepper

1) Boil the potatoes. When tender, drain and slice them.
2) Shake the remaining ingredients in a screw-topped jar. Pour over the still warm potatoes and toss. Serve warm or chill until serving.

Patates Salatası II

This potato salad is slightly spicy but shouldn't be overpowering so, choose mild chillies. Shallots are probably closer in flavour to the small tasty (but not hot) onions found in Turkish salads. If you can't get any, use spring onions (scallions) or a quarter of a Spanish onion.

450g/1lb/2½ cups	small potatoes
1	large shallot
	or
2	small shallots, peeled, halved and thinly sliced
1	mild chilli, deseeded and quartered
1	slightly under-ripe tomato, quartered
3 tbsp	extra virgin olive oil
	juice of 1 lemon
3 tbsp	parsley
	salt and pepper

1) Boil the potatoes. When tender, drain and cube them. Add the shallots.
2) Whizz the remaining ingredients in a liquidizer. Pour over the potatoes and shallots. Serve warm or chill until needed.

Patlıcan Salatası Yoğurtlu

This is very similar to Patlıcan Salatası (see page 37) but do try both, the differences are worth exploring.

2	medium aubergines (eggplants)
1	small red (bell) pepper
4	moderately hot green chillies e.g. Anaheim
	or
4	canned chillies
2 tbsp	olive oil
1 tbsp	lemon juice
2 cloves	garlic, crushed
½ tsp	salt
150g/5½ oz/¾ cup	plain yoghurt

1) Place the aubergines (eggplants), (bell) pepper and chillies under a hot grill (broiler). Turn until the skins blacken and the aubergines (eggplants) are soft. Peel, discarding the pepper seeds.
2) Purée the aubergines (eggplants), 2 chillies, olive oil, lemon juice, garlic and salt. When fairly smooth, add the yoghurt and whizz very briefly to combine.
3) Scrape into a dish and decorate with strips of the red pepper and the remaining chillies, sliced. Leave in the refrigerator and serve when ready.

Patlıcan ve Domates Salatası

This aubergine (eggplant) and tomato salad works brilliantly because the richness of the fried aubergine (eggplant) is cut by the fresh tomato sauce on top.

1	large aubergine (eggplant), sliced 0.5cm/ ¼ inch thick
	oil
2	large tomatoes, chopped
2 cloves	garlic, crushed
	salt and pepper
a pinch	sugar
1 tbsp	chopped parsley

1) Fry the aubergine (eggplant) slices in hot oil until nicely browned on both sides. Lay on a plate.
2) Mix together the tomatoes, garlic, salt, pepper and sugar. Spoon over the aubergine (eggplant). Top with the parsley. Chill until required.

Patlıcan Salatası

It's easy to mistake this aubergine (eggplant) salad for humus – it
has almost the same appearance at first glance – but the flavour
and texture are very different. If you are having a barbecue, roast
the aubergine (eggplant) over the charcoal instead of in the oven
– it is faster and you get a lovely smoky taste.

2	large aubergines (eggplants)
	or
4	smaller aubergines (eggplants) – smaller ones cook faster
4 tbsp	extra virgin olive oil
1	lemon, cut 1 slice from the centre for garnish
	salt
a few	black olives
a few sprigs	parsley

1) Place the aubergines (eggplants) in the hottest oven. Turn
   occasionally and bake until soft. Depending on size, this takes
   about 15 minutes.
2) Peel and place in a food processor with the oil, lemon juice and
   a good pinch of salt. Process in bursts to get a fairly smooth
   purée.
3) Scrape into a dish. Decorate with the lemon slice, black olives
   and parsley.

Soğanlı Salatası

The onions in this salad are made sweetly mild by kneading them with salt. This salad makes a great relish with other egg or cheese dishes.

3	medium onions, thinly sliced in rings
2 tsp	salt
4 tbsp	olive oil
	juice of a lemon
	or
3 tbsp	white wine vinegar
2 tbsp	chopped parsley

1) Put the onions in a large bowl, separating out all the rings. Sprinkle with the salt. Work the salt into the onions with your hands, pressing and turning as if you were kneading bread. Rinse very well then stand in a colander with a weight on it, to drain.

2) Combine the oil and lemon juice or vinegar. Spread the onions out on a plate. Drizzle over the dressing, mix well and scatter over the parsley.

Tarator

You have to like walnuts and garlic for this salad contains little else. Stalls and booths set up in the street and proclaim 'Tarator' on hand-painted signs. Turks eat it by the handful. I prefer it over a green salad (Yeşil Salata, see page 41), a yoghurt-based salad or grilled vegetables. On its own it makes my tongue prickle! A very similar salad is found in the south of France, both rely on fresh walnuts. Late Autumn is therefore the best time to make Tarator – check the packing date. Shelling your own walnuts of course is best, but would take too long.

2 bulbs	garlic
125g/4oz/a good cup	ground walnuts
90ml/3fl oz/⅓ cup	sesame oil (the untoasted sort)
90ml/3fl oz/⅓ cup	lemon juice
60g/2oz/1 cup	finely chopped parsley
1–2 slices	lemon

1) Push the garlic cloves through a garlic press – there is no need to peel. The garlic is squeezed through the holes, leaving the papery skin behind for you to discard and then you put the next clove in.
2) Whizz the garlic, walnuts, oil and lemon juice in bursts in a food processor until well amalgamated. Add the parsley and whizz again briefly to mix. Scrape into a bowl and top with the lemon slices. Chill until required.

Tere Salatası

This is probably the simplest recipe in the book – it is a rocket (arugula) salad. It is a true salad in that the word derives from the Latin for salt and was used to describe greens etc. eaten with salt. If you have never tried the dark, peppery leaves of rocket (arugula) you are in for a real treat. Most supermarkets and good greengrocers sell ready-washed bags of leaves – but it is very easy to grow too, it comes up like cress and can be snipped off quite young. However the older the leaves, the pokier the flavour.

> 250g/8oz/4 cups   rocket leaves
> salt
> a little   extra virgin olive oil

1) Toss the leaves with a good pinch of salt and drizzle with a little oil just before serving.

Yeşil Salata

A green salad with a bit of bite!

90g/3oz/¾ cup	spring onions (scallions), roughly chopped
1	moderately hot green chilli, deseeded
3 tbsp	olive oil
	juice of 1 lemon
a good pinch	salt
1	cos (romaine) lettuce, shredded

1) Put the spring onions (scallions), chilli, olive oil, lemon juice and salt in a food processor. Using the pulse button, whizz until an emulsified dressing with finely chopped spring onions (scallions) and chillies is formed.
2) Pour over the lettuce and toss. Serve.

Yoğurtlu Semizotu

This is a tangy refreshing yoghurt-based salad. It contains purslane. With the advent of the designer salad greens in supermarkets, purslane can now be occasionally found. If it is not available, use 2 bunches of watercress instead. The flavour won't be the same but it is very good also.

200g/7oz/1 cup	yoghurt
2–3 cloves	garlic, crushed
5 tsp	salt
225g/8oz/3–4 cups	purslane leaves – discard the stems or use them for something else

1) Mix the yoghurt, garlic and salt together, then carefully stir in the purslane until well coated. Leave in the refrigerator until ready to serve.

Zeytin Salatası

There are often olive salads in the meze chill cabinet, but this one is my favourite. For best colour, don't mix together too soon.

175g/6oz/1 cup	black olives
2 tbsp	capers
3	hard-boiled eggs, peeled and diced – nice chunky pieces
2	tomatoes, cubed
1	lemon, cut into wedges
1 tbsp	chopped parsley

1) Simply mix together, topping with the lemon wedges and parsley. You don't need salt as the olives are already very salty.

Zeytinyağli Enginar

Artichokes in olive oil – can be served still warm or, more traditionally, cold.

125ml/5fl oz/²/₃ cup	olive oil
	juice of 1 lemon
225g/8oz/2 cups	small shallots, peeled and trimmed
2 sticks	celery, sliced
2	carrots, sliced
	salt and pepper
1 large can	artichoke bottoms – about 6–8, rinsed and drained
a handful	fresh dill or fennel

1) Put the oil, lemon juice, shallots, celery and carrots in a pan. Season well and simmer for 15 minutes.
2) Add the artichokes and cook for another 10 minutes. Place in a dish and scatter on the dill or fennel. Serve when you are ready.

Zeytinyağli Pırasa

The Yalcin restaurant, tucked at the far end of Dalyan's riverside esplanade may not have had a huge range of mezes but they did have some great ones, including these leeks in olive oil. They become so meltingly soft but not wet or mushy. Use baby leeks for speed, they require less cleaning.

This is another dish that is supposed to be served cold but is extremely good hot as well.

60ml/2fl oz/¼ cup	olive oil
450g/1lb/4 cups	baby leeks, washed and cut into 2.5cm/1 inch lengths
2 cloves	garlic, thinly sliced
125g/4oz/1 cup	baby carrots, sliced
125ml/4½fl oz/½ cup	water
a pinch	sugar
	salt and pepper

1) Place the oil, leeks and garlic in a saucepan – a frying pan isn't suitable. Fry gently for 5 minutes.
2) Add the carrots, water, sugar and seasonings. Cover and simmer for 20 minutes. Serve or chill until required.

Zeytinyağli Taze Fasulye

Green beans in olive oil – serve still warm with a topping of crumbled white cheese for a complete meal or, cold as part of a meze spread.

60ml/2fl oz/¼ cup	olive oil
450g/1lb/5 cups	French beans, topped and tailed
2	onions, chopped
2	medium tomatoes, chopped
	or
200g/7oz can	chopped tomatoes
a good pinch	sugar
	pepper and salt
250ml/9fl oz/1 cup	water

1) Heat the oil then throw in the beans and onions. Cover and shake the pan from time to time. Cook for 3 minutes then add the tomatoes, sugar, seasonings and water.
2) Simmer for 15 minutes. Serve hot or chill until required.

Cook's Note
Runner, wax, Helda or flat beans can all be used. Cut into 5cm/ 2 inch lengths and cook until tender.

Zeytinyağli Bakla

Use this recipe in the late spring when broad beans are fresh and tiny and they haven't grown those grey overcoats. When they are bigger they take significantly longer than 30 minutes to cook. You will need about 1.5kg/3lb/7½ cups unshelled weight – delegate the podding!

60ml/2fl oz/¼ cup	olive oil
1	red onion, finely chopped
450g/1lb/4 cups	shelled broad beans
1 tsp	sugar
300ml/11fl oz/1¼ cups	water
	salt
2 tbsp	chopped dill or fennel

1) Heat the oil and fry the onion. When soft, add the beans and sugar. Cook for 5 minutes.
2) Add the water and simmer for 15 minutes or until tender. Season well. Place in a dish and scatter with the dill or fennel. Serve when you are ready.

Hot Meze

Enginar Dolması

These are stuffed artichokes but you can try the same filling to stuff kohlrabi or turnips. Peel and parboil the kohlrabi or turnips, halve and hollow out the centre with a melon baller then use instead of the artichoke bottoms. As they are not available ready-prepared, they will take a little longer than 30 minutes.

2 tbsp	butter or margarine
2	onions, chopped
200g/7oz can	chopped tomatoes
75g/3oz/scant ½ cup	rice
75g/3oz/½ cup	peas, shelled or frozen
125ml/4fl oz/½ cup	boiling water
8	canned artichoke bottoms, drained
2	egg yolks
1 tbsp	lemon juice
4 tbsp	water
	black pepper

1) Melt the butter or margarine and quickly fry the onions. Add the tomatoes, rice and peas. Cook for 1 minute, then add the water. Cover and cook for 10 minutes.
2) Fill the artichokes with the rice mixture. Place in a baking dish.
3) Whisk together the egg yolks, lemon juice, water and black pepper. Dribble over the artichokes, cover and bake at 200°C/400°F/Gas Mark 6 for 10 minutes. Serve hot or cold.

Etsiz Patlıcan Dolması

Hot stuffed vegetables almost invariably contain meat in Turkey, cold ones rarely do. They are prefixed with *'etli'* meaning 'with meat'. That fount of much useful knowledge, *The Rough Guide to Turkey*, tells me that *'etsiz'* means 'without meat', hence our contrived title! Stuffed aubergines (eggplants) come in many guises but unfortunately a large number of the recipes take far too long to feature in this book.

4	small aubergines (eggplants) – about 12.5cm/5 inches long
	oil
2	onions, chopped
2 cloves	garlic
1 tsp	cumin
375g/12oz can	Italian or continental lentils – the grey ones
200g/7oz can	chopped tomatoes
	salt and pepper

1) Put the aubergines (eggplants) in a hot oven, about 200°C/400°F/Gas Mark 6, until softening – around 10 minutes, depending on size.
2) Meanwhile heat 2 tablespoons of oil in a pan and fry the onion and garlic until nicely golden. Add the cumin.
3) Halve the aubergines (eggplants) lengthways and make criss-cross lines across the flesh. Scoop out and chop. Add to the onions, fry for 1 minute. Add the lentils. Pile into the aubergine (eggplant) skins.

4) Place in a baking dish and top with the tomatoes. Season and dribble with a little oil. Bake at 230°C/450°F/Gas Mark 8 for 10 minutes. Serve.

Fırında Patates

These are baked potatoes but not jacket potatoes as we are familiar with them. Use tiny potatoes, about the size of quail's eggs or just a touch larger. These are so good and require no effort or care, you will make them again and again. Cook twice as many and pig out! If you are worried about the cholesterol levels, use a good vegetable margarine or, better still flavourwise, 1 tablespoon of butter and 1 tablespoon of olive oil.

2 tbsp   butter
450g/1lb/3 cups   tiny potatoes

1) Melt the butter in a cast iron casserole dish. Turn the potatoes about in it. Cover and place in a hot oven – 230°C/450°F/Gas Mark 8 – for 20 minutes. Stir around and serve.

Cook's Note
You can add herbs, seasoning etc. but I prefer them absolutely plain. When there are no small potatoes, use waxy large ones, cubed. They are not as good but then that still leaves room for several levels of seriously deliciousness.

Ispanakli Böreği

You may have come across the Greek version of this, Spanakopita. Different cooks use varying amounts of cheese; some use none, substituting yoghurt. It can also be made with an added eggy filling as in Peynirli Tepsi Böreği (see page 69). Use a big wide pastry brush and you can do this in 30 minutes – just don't be too finicky. (Slip, slap, slop then close the oven door, take a breath, relax and make a salad!)

125g/4oz/½ cup	butter or margarine, melted
1	onion, chopped
1 clove	garlic, crushed
500g/1lb 2oz/9 cups	ready-washed spinach
200g/7oz/1 cup	firm white cheese, crumbled
a few	pink peppercorns, crushed
	salt and pepper
350g	filo pastry

1) Put 2 tablespoons of the butter or margarine in a pan. Fry the onion and garlic quickly until colouring.
2) Add the spinach, tossing like a salad to coat in the hot butter. Cook, stirring, for 5 minutes.
3) Add the cheese and season with the pink peppercorns, salt (if necessary) and black pepper.
4) Line a lasagne dish with a sheet of filo, brush it with melted butter and cover with another sheet. Repeat 3 times, then spread over the spinach. Cover with more filo, brushing and layering 3 times.
5) Bake at 230°C/450°F/Gas Mark 8 for 20 minutes. Serve.

Kabak Musakka

This is a courgette (zucchini) moussaka but, unlike the perhaps more familiar Greek version, there is no cheese sauce and it doesn't require baking in the oven – although you can if you prefer, do the final cooking in a fairly hot oven.

Serve with a bowl of grated cheese if liked and bread or rice.

4	large courgettes (zucchini), thickly sliced
3	red onions, quartered
1 clove	garlic, quartered
125g/4oz/1 cup	mushrooms
2 tbsp	butter or margarine
200g/7oz can	chopped tomatoes
	salt and pepper
1 tbsp	chopped dill
1 tbsp	chopped mint

1) Boil or steam the courgette (zucchini) slices for 5 minutes. Drain.
2) Meanwhile, chop the onion, garlic and mushrooms together in a food processor to give a fine mince. Scrape out and fry in the butter or margarine on a fairly high heat until colouring. Add the tomatoes, season well and cook stirring until thick.
3) Cover the base of a flameproof casserole with half the courgette (zucchini) slices. Top with half the tomato mixture and repeat. Sprinkle over the herbs. Cover tightly and cook for 15 minutes.

Karnıbahar Pane

These are cauliflower fritters and can be made in smaller quantities to use up any leftover vegetables (carrots, broccoli, peas etc.) that you may have lurking in the refrigerator.

1	small cauliflower
1	small onion, chopped
2 tbsp	butter or margarine
2 tbsp	plain flour
125ml/4fl oz/½ cup	milk
125g/4oz/2 cups	fresh breadcrumbs
	oil for deep-frying

1) Break up the cauliflower into florets and boil until tender. Drain.
2) Meanwhile, fry the onion in the butter or margarine until softening. Stir in the flour and cook over a low heat for 2 minutes. Stir in the milk and cook, stirring until very thick.
3) Mix in the cooked cauliflower. Spread the breadcrumbs out on a plate. Drop tablespoonfuls of the cauliflower mixture onto the breadcrumbs. Gently pat down to form thick 'cakes'. Turn and gently press into the breadcrumbs to coat the other side. Leave in a cold place until needed.
4) Deep-fry in a heavy skillet or similar pan until crisp and golden on both sides – take care when turning. Serve at once.

Cook's Note
These fritters can be shallow-fried in oil or butter or baked in a hot oven on a well greased baking sheet.

Lahmacun

Turkey's round pizza, Lahmacun, is usually made with spiced ground meat. You can add some tomato purée (paste) to the topping if you must, but do try it without first.

350g/12oz/2½ cups	strong plain flour
1 tbsp	instant dried yeast
½ tsp	salt
200ml/7fl oz/¾ cup	warm water
1	red onion, quartered
125g/4oz/1 cup	chestnut (brown cap) mushrooms
1 clove	garlic
1	small, moderately hot, chilli, deseeded
	olive oil
	salt and black pepper
4 tbsp	fresh chopped parsley

1) In a food processor, using the dough attachment, knead the flour, yeast, salt and warm water until a soft smooth dough is formed – about 3–4 minutes. Add a little more flour if necessary to prevent stickiness. (If making the dough by hand it will take longer.)
2) Using the chopping blade in the processor, mince the onion, mushrooms, garlic and chilli with 1 tablespoon of olive oil.
3) Divide the dough into 4, press or roll out to 20cm/8 inch circles on heavy, oiled baking sheets. Cover with the minced onion mixture, pressing it into the dough. Dust with salt and a generous grinding of black pepper. Drizzle with olive oil.

4) Bake in the hottest oven you can – turn it right up as high as it will go. This should take about 10 minutes – bases will be crisp and golden around the edges. Scatter over the parsley and serve.

Mantar Pane

These deep-fried garlic mushrooms go very well with the spicier meze, especially Ezme Acili (see page 18).

200g/7oz/1 cup	white cheese, crumbled
2 cloves	garlic, crushed
350g/12oz/3 cups	firm mushrooms – caps only, ideal size 3.5cm/1½ inches
2	eggs
100g/3oz/2 cups	fresh breadcrumbs
	oil for deep-frying

1) Mash together the cheese and garlic with a fork. Press a bit into every mushroom cup.
2) Beat the eggs in a deep bowl. Put the breadcrumbs in a bag.
3) Drop the filled mushrooms a few at a time into the eggs, then put them in the bag. Trapping some air inside, seal the bag and shake to coat the mushrooms in breadcrumbs.
4) Fry the coated mushrooms in hot oil while egging and bread-crumbing the rest. Serve hot.

Mantar ve Pırasa Şiş

Mushroom kebabs vary enormously depending on the mushrooms used. For large, dark, flat field mushrooms, use a good red wine or balsamic vinegar and serve with Kuskus (see page 92) or bread. For closed cap, cultivated mushrooms use the lemon juice and serve with plain rice mixed with chopped parsley. If you don't have leeks, use onions.

375g/12oz/3 cups	mushrooms, cut large ones into cubes
2	leeks, cleaned and cut into 2cm/1 inch lengths
2 tbsp	vinegar or lemon juice (see above)
4 tbsp	oil
6	pink peppercorns, crushed
	salt

1) Thread the mushrooms and leeks onto skewers. (Thread the leeks crosswise through the rings.)
2) Mix together the remaining ingredients and brush over the skewers. Leave in a cool place until needed.
3) Grill (broil), turning from time to time, until the leeks are browned and the mushroom juices run. Serve.

Cook's Note
Have a pan beneath the kebabs to catch the wonderful juices. Drizzle over the kebabs.

Mücver

A favourite of Sophie and Tom, who we met on the boat on Lake Köycegiz and a way of serving courgettes (zucchini) that my children approve. I think these thin pancake-like fritters are great with the fiery Ezme Acili (see page 18). A food processor makes light work of both recipes.

900g/2lb/8 cups	courgettes (zucchini), grated (shredded)
1	large Spanish onion, grated (shredded)
150g/5oz/1 cup	firm white cheese, crumbled or finely grated (shredded)
150g/5oz/1 cup	plain flour
3	large eggs
2 tbsp	chopped dill
	salt and pepper
	olive oil

1) Mix everything except the oil together, seasoning well.
2) Heat 1cm/½ inch of oil in a heavy based pan. Drop the mixture by tablespoonfuls, flattening if necessary. Flip and brown the other side, drain, sprinkle with salt and serve.

Nohut Guveç

Nohut are chick peas (garbanzos) and a guveç is a casserole that has a gravy with it as opposed to kebap (see page 65) which is thicker. A lidded flameproof casserole dish is necessary. Ready-prepared vegetables – fresh or frozen – will speed you on your way.

4 tbsp	oil
125g/4oz/1 cup	okra (lady's fingers), trimmed
1	medium aubergine (eggplant), diced
125g/4oz/1 cup	baby carrots, trimmed
125g/4oz/1 cup	French beans
400g/14oz can	chick peas (garbanzos), rinsed and drained
200g/7oz can	chopped tomatoes
1	small green (bell) pepper, sliced
250ml/9fl oz/1 cup	vegetable stock or water
2 cloves	garlic, crushed
	salt and pepper
125g/4oz/1 cup	small (pickling) onions or shallots, peeled and trimmed
1 tbsp	butter or margarine

1) Stand the casserole dish over a moderate heat. Pour in the oil. Layer in the vegetables in the order in which they are given.
2) Mix together the stock or water and garlic, seasoning well. Pour over the casserole. Top with the onions and butter or margarine. Cover and transfer to a hot oven, 230°C/450°F/ Gas Mark 8 for 20–25 minutes until the vegetables are tender. Serve with rice.

Patatas Böreği

This is a version of pies we ate on the beach in Alanya – the same cheese and potato filling is found in filo wrapping too. Any leftover cooked potatoes can be used: boiled work best but baked, roasted, fried or even mashed can be used. If using mashed, simmer the onions in the milk and add the potato with the cheese – the texture is not as good but it is still tasty and filling.

250ml/9fl oz/1 cup	milk
2	onions, quartered and sliced
2	large cooked potatoes, quartered and sliced
1 tsp	pink peppercorns, crushed
1	bay leaf
125g/4oz/1 cup	Kasar or Cheddar cheese, grated
2 × 25cm/10 inches diameter circles	ready-rolled puff or flaky pastry

1) Put the milk, onions, potatoes, peppercorns and bay leaf into a pan and simmer together for 7 minutes.
2) Place 1 pastry circle in the base of a pie dish. Damp the edges. Stir the cheese into the potato/milk mixture and pour into the pie dish. Cover with the second pastry circle. Seal edges.
3) Bake for 20 minutes at 230°C/450°F/Gas Mark 8, until the pastry is puffed and browned. Serve in wedges.

Cook's Note
The ready-rolled pastry saves time but any good puff pastry can be used.

Patates Köftesi

Köfte are balls or rissoles, sometimes fried and sometimes poached. Many traditionally contain meat but not in this case, these are potato balls. Use a pressure cooker, microwave or just cut the potatoes small to save time. At a pinch you can use instant mash, but the results are not as good.

525g/18oz/3 cups	potatoes, mashed
2	egg yolks
3 tbsp	plain flour
½ tsp	salt
	pepper
½ tsp	chilli powder
1	egg, beaten
	oil for deep-frying
1 tbsp	chopped parsley

1) Mix the egg yolks into the potato. Form into egg shaped balls.
2) Combine the flour and seasonings. Roll the potato balls in the flour. Dip them in the beaten egg then re-roll in the flour.
3) Deep-fry in the hot oil until crisp and golden. Drain and serve, scattered with parsley.

Patlıcan Kebap

This aubergine (eggplant) kebap is a bit like a rich, baked rata-touille. The high temperature of the oven brings out the very savoury notes of the vegetables. The best kebap I've ever eaten was at the Gaziantep restaurant in Alanya. What a pleasure to just sit and watch the very professional waiters buzzing about with plates and plates of wonderful food, some flaming as they passed. Pure theatre, just like the bustle of Parisian institutions such as Chartier Montmarte. Gaziantep, an industrial town, in eastern Turkey, above Syria, is not only famous for its pistachios but, like the Hatay below it, for the hotter, spicier nature of its kebaps. If you are not keen on chillies, simply leave them out – they do at most points west of Antalya!

Heavy, flat terracotta or cast iron dishes are needed – individual ones cook within the allotted time but larger ones will take longer.

4 tbsp	olive oil
2	red onions, chopped
1	chilli, chopped
2 cloves	garlic, chopped
2	aubergines (eggplants), cubed
2	courgettes (zucchini), cubed
400g/14oz can	chopped tomatoes
	salt and pepper
1 tsp	sugar
125g/4oz/1 cup	Dil or mozzarella cheese, diced
2 tbsp	chopped parsley

1) Heat the oil in a heavy pan. Fry the onion, chilli and garlic until softening.

2) Keep the heat quite high. Add the aubergines (eggplants) and fry, stirring, until it begins to brown. Add the courgettes (zucchini) and stir-fry until they begin to take a little colour. Quickly add the tomatoes and season well with salt, pepper and sugar. Cook for 2 more minutes.

3) Divide between 4 heavy ovenproof dishes. Bake at 230°C/450°F/Gas Mark 8 for 15 minutes. Scatter on the cheese and cook for another 5 minutes. Serve with a sprinkle of parsley.

Patlıcan ve Biber Şiş

This is what most of us recognize as a kebab – aubergine (egg-plant) and pepper cubes on skewers. Serve on a lovely bed of pilav. Even nicer cooked on a barbecue.

2	large aubergines (eggplants), cubed
8	long green mild peppers, cubed
	or
2	green (bell) peppers, cubed
3	red (bell) peppers, cubed
3	red onions, peeled and quartered
1 tbsp	tomato purée (paste)
3 tbsp	olive oil
1 tbsp	red wine vinegar
a good pinch	dried thyme
	salt and pepper

1) Thread the vegetables onto the skewers, having cut the onion quarters in half crossways.
2) Mix together the tomato purée (paste), oil, vinegar, thyme and seasonings. Brush all over the skewers of vegetables. Leave in a cool place until ready.
3) Grill (broil) until browned and tender, turning occasionally. Serve.

Patlıcan Beğendi

This is another sort of aubergine (eggplant) purée, this time it is hot and is usually served as a side dish with a rich kebap or guvec. However, it makes a great supper dish with good bread and a tomato salad.

2	long, thin aubergines (eggplants)
2 tbsp	butter or margarine
2 tbsp	plain flour
375ml/13fl oz/1½ cups	milk
	salt and pepper
90g/3oz/1 cup	Kasar or Emmental cheese, grated

1) Bake the aubergines (eggplants) in a hot oven – 230°C/450°F/Gas Mark 8 – until soft, about 15 minutes.
2) Meanwhile, melt the butter, stir in the flour and cook over a low heat for 5 minutes. Remove from the heat and gradually add the milk.
3) Cook, stirring, until the mixture is very smooth and thick. Season well.
4) Peel the baked aubergines (eggplants) and mash. Beat in the thick white sauce and cheese. Serve hot.

Peynirli Tepsi Böreği

125g/4oz/½ cup	butter, melted
3 tbsp	yoghurt
250ml/9fl oz/1 cup	milk
3	eggs
	salt and pepper
350g packet	filo pastry
350g/12oz/3 cups	white cheese, crumbled
3 tbsp	chopped parsley
3 tbsp	chopped dill
1	egg yolk, to glaze

1) Brush a Swiss (jelly) roll tin with a little of the melted butter. Combine the rest of the butter, yoghurt, milk and eggs. Season.

2) Lay a sheet of filo over the base of the tin. Cover with some of the butter/milk mixture. Top with another layer of filo, a covering of butter/milk and a further layer of filo.

3) Scatter over the cheese. Cover with the herbs then another sheet of filo. Repeat the butter/milk and filo layers until the mixture is used up, ending with a filo sheet. Brush the top with the yolk and bake at 190°C/375°F/Gas Mark 5 for 20 minutes, until golden.

Peynirli Kadayif

Kadayif is the same as konafa, the thin vermicelli-looking pastry available in some delicatessens. If you cannot find it, use several buttered sheets of filo (see Ispanakli Böreği recipe on page 54) top and bottom instead. This pie can be eaten hot or cold.

350g/12oz/2–3 cups	kadayif pastry (cup quantity used depends on how compacted it is)
175g/6oz/³⁄₄ cup	butter or margarine, melted
350g/12oz/1½ cups	cottage or curd cheese
4 tbsp	grated Parmesan cheese
3	medium eggs
15g/½oz/1 cup	mint leaves
½ tsp	pink peppercorns, crushed
	salt

1) Put the kadayif in a large bowl. Pour over the butter or margarine. Using two forks, lightly and quickly lift and toss the strands to coat and separate them.
2) Place the remaining ingredients in a food processor and whizz until smooth.
3) Press half the kadayif into the base of a 18cm/7 inches diameter deep cake tin or soufflé dish. Scrape on the cheese mixture. Top with the remaining kadayif.
4) Bake for 25 minutes at 230°C/450°F/Gas Mark 8 until the filling is set and the kadayif has browned.

Puf Böreği

This recipe sounds involved and complicated but it isn't. Many hands, well 2 pairs anyway, make fast work. One rolls and shapes while the other fries. Other shortcuts are to use cottage cheese with garlic and herbs already added or ready-rolled flaky pastry – don't use puff, it spits and twists and is too greasy. However you do it, it is possible to do it in 30 minutes – I did the first batch, on my own, in under 25.

Other fillings can be used. The Natural restaurant in Dalyan uses a similar filling to the Patatas Böreği (see page 63) and one that seems to be made with thick cheese sauce and peas. There they dip the pasties in egg and breadcrumb first before deep-frying – a touch over-egging the böreği I think.

300g/10oz/2 cups	strong plain flour
1	egg
1 tbsp	yoghurt
2 tbsp	soft margarine
50ml/scant 2fl oz/scant ¼ cup	water
200g/7oz/1 cup	goat's cheese, crumbled
1 clove	garlic, crushed
2 tbsp	chopped parsley
	oil for deep-frying

1) Put the flour, egg, yoghurt and half the margarine in a food processor with the dough attachment. Run until well mixed. Through the lid, pour on the water until it forms a soft ball. Run a minute longer.

2) Divide the dough into 4 balls. Roll each out to 20cm/8 inches across. Smear the tops of 3 of them with the remaining margarine. Stack on top of each other, ending with the ungreased one.

3) Roll out to 50cm/20 inches across. Stamp out circles with a 10cm/4 inch cutter. Damp one side of the circle.

4) Mix together the cheese, garlic and parsley. Pinch together a small pile and put it on a dough round. Fold over and press the edges together to seal.

5) Deep-fry in hot oil until crisp and golden, turning once. Serve hot or cold.

Saç Kavurma

This is a Turkish 'stir-fry' or 'balti' – authentically it does contain meat, but not much. Vary the vegetables according to what is in season. The kavurma (pan), tends to be heavier than the average wok, it is more like an Indian karhai but either can be used, or if unavailable use a large heavy skillet.

2 tbsp	olive oil
1	chilli, deseeded and chopped
1	red onion, sliced
2	large potatoes, cubed
1 tsp	ground cumin
1	bay leaf
a good pinch	cayenne
	salt and pepper
1 clove	garlic, sliced
2	red (bell) peppers, sliced
2	courgettes (zucchini), cubed

1) Heat the oil in the pan (see above). Fry the chilli and onion quickly until softening. Add the potatoes and fry, stirring, until they begin to colour.
2) Add the remaining ingredients and stir-fry until all of the vegetables are tender. Serve.

Sebze Kizartması

These are vegetable fritters, you can use most vegetables including aubergines (eggplants), courgettes (zucchini), carrots, mushrooms, asparagus, cauliflower, broccoli or beans. Remember to slice thin and lengthways (button mushrooms, asparagus and beans excepted). You want a high surface area to volume ratio: that is, lots of crunchy outside!

Turkish beer is light, so most American beers are suitable. Use lager in the UK.

4	tomatoes, chopped
	or
250ml/9fl oz/1 cup	passata (Italian strained tomatoes)
250g/9oz/1 cup	yoghurt
1 tbsp	chopped parsley
2 cloves	garlic, crushed
150g/5oz/1 cup	plain flour
1 tsp	chilli powder
	salt and pepper
250ml/9fl oz/1 cup	beer (see above)
450g/1lb	chosen vegetables, sliced (see above)
	oil for deep-frying

1) Put the tomatoes or passata (Italian strained tomatoes) into a bowl. In a separate bowl, mix the yoghurt, parsley and garlic. Put in a cool place.
2) In a blender, combine the flour, chilli powder, salt, pepper and beer, whizzing only enough to make a smooth batter.

3) Dip the vegetable slices in the batter and deep-fry until crisp and golden. Serve with the tomatoes and yoghurt sauces.

Sigara Böreği

The first time we went to Turkey we were amazed to find unappetizingly titled Cigarette Pie on the menu, but were delighted to discover these crisp golden fingers of pastry rolled around white cheese.

300g/10oz/1½ cups	firm white cheese, crumbled or finely grated
2 tbsp	finely grated Parmesan (optional)
1	egg white
2 tbsp	chopped parsley
2 tbsp	chopped dill
350g packet	filo pastry – approx. 10 sheets, 20cm × 15cm/ 8 inches x 6 inches
	oil

1) Mix together the cheese(s), egg white and herbs, mashing well with a fork.
2) Cut the filo sheets in half crossways. Place a line of filling along the short edge of a sheet. Fold the long sides in and roll up tightly, lightly damping the end to seal. Repeat.
3) Shallow fry in hot oil until crisp and golden. Alternatively, brush with oil and bake in a hot oven or deep-fry.

Terbiyeli Kereviz

Egg and lemon sauce is wonderful over braised celeriac. The same sauce can be used over celery hearts, now available in some supermarkets. Celeriac is one of my favourite vegetables and I was delighted to find it in Turkish cooking. I wasn't, however, convinced by a recipe that teamed it with dessicated coconut and yoghurt.

Broccoli and asparagus are both delicious cooked this way.

3	small celeriac – no larger than tennis ball size – peeled and sliced, 0.5cm/¼ inch thick
2 tbsp	butter
2	onions, chopped
2 tbsp	plain flour
1 litre/1¾ pints/4 cups	water
	salt and pepper
2	lemons – 1 quartered, 1 squeezed
2	eggs, beaten

1) In a large, heavy pan, fry the celeriac gently in the butter, turning about to coat all the slices. Add the onions and flour, tossing to coat. Pour on the water and add the quartered lemon. Season well.
2) Bring to the boil, stirring occasionally. Simmer until tender, about 15 minutes. Using a slotted spoon, remove the celeriac slices and arrange on a plate.
3) Strain off 250ml/9fl oz/1 cup of the cooking liquid into a clean pan. Whisk the lemon juice and eggs together thoroughly,

then whisk into the saucepan. Keep whisking over a low heat until the mixture thickens. Pour over the celeriac and serve.

Cook's Note
Save the extra cooking liquid, it is a well flavoured stock. If not required straightaway, you can freeze for later use.

Tereyağli Mantar Kiremit

These are baked, stuffed mushrooms, cooked traditionally in small, heavy, flat terracotta dishes. They are Turkish 'Garlic Mushrooms'.

60g/2oz/¼ cup	butter
2 cloves	garlic, crushed
125g/4oz/1 cup	Kasar or Cheddar cheese, grated
350g/12oz/3 cups	mushrooms, caps only – use the stalks for stock
1 tbsp	chopped parsley

1) Very liberally butter 4 small or 1 large ovenproof dish.
2) Mix the garlic and cheese together. Press a pinch of this mixture into each mushroom. Place on the butter, cheese-side up. Cover with aluminium foil.
3) Bake for 10 minutes at 220°C/425°F/Gas Mark 7. Serve hot with a scattering of parsley.

Pasta, Rice and
Other Grains

Bakla Pilavı

This broad bean and rice dish is also known as an Azerbaijani pilav.

300g/11oz/2 cups	long grain rice
2 tbsp	salt
	boiling water
3 tbsp	butter or margarine
750ml/1¾ pints/3 cups	water or stock
400g/14oz can	broad beans, drained
	juice of 1 lemon
2 tbsp	chopped dill

1) Put the rice and salt into a bowl. Cover with the boiling water and leave for 10 minutes. Rinse and drain thoroughly.
2) Melt the butter or margarine and fry the rice for 7 minutes, stirring often.
3) While the rice is frying, heat the water or stock, broad beans and lemon juice.
4) Pour the broad beans and cooking liquid into the rice. Stir around and cook over a moderate heat until the liquid has all been absorbed.
5) Stir through the dill and serve.

Bulgur Pilavı

Bulgur, or Bulgar wheat as it is labelled in most supermarkets, has already been partly cooked. The grains are cracked by boiling and then dried. To speed preparation time, you can soak the wheat in the morning before you go out. Drain it and leave it covered in the fridge all day. Make double quantities and freeze half for use in stuffing vegetables, see Dolması (pages 50 and 51).

175g/6oz/1 cup	bulgar wheat
500ml/18fl oz/2 cups	boiling water
2 tbsp	oil
1	small onion, sliced
125g/4oz/1 cup	oyster mushrooms (pleurots), sliced
4 tbsp	raisins
3 tbsp	shelled pumpkin seeds
2 tbsp	sesame seeds
2 tbsp	shelled pistachios
2 tbsp	pine kernels
1 tbsp	ground cinnamon
	salt and pepper
2 tbsp	chopped parsley

1) Place the bulgar in a bowl and pour on the boiling water. Leave for 15 minutes.
2) Heat the oil and fry the onion and oyster mushrooms for a couple of minutes. Add the raisins, seeds, pistachios, pine kernels and cinnamon. Fry for another minute.

3) Drain any excess water from the bulgar and add to the pan. Stir-fry until well mixed and hot through. Season and stir in the parsley. Serve.

Bulgar Pilavı II

This pilav is almost risotto-like. The coarseness of the bulgar means it is not creamy like a real risotto, but it has a somewhat soupy or porridgy nature.

Use an accompaniment to şiş (see pages 60 and 67) or double the quantities and serve with grated Cheddar or crumbled white cheese for a simple meal.

175g/6oz/1 cup	bulgar wheat
500ml/18fl oz/2 cups	boiling water
1	onion, chopped
1	small chilli, chopped
1 tbsp	olive oil
200g/7oz can	chopped tomatoes
	salt and pepper

1) Put the bulgar in a bowl and pour on the boiling water.
2) Fry the onion and chilli in the oil until softening. Add the tomatoes and the soaking bulgar and water. Season. Simmer, stirring occasionally, for 15 minutes. Serve.

Domates Dolması

These are baked, stuffed tomatoes. Do not forget to scoop the cooking liquor all over them before serving.

If you can find the large irregularly-shaped but delicious Marmande tomatoes you will only need 1 each instead of 2.

100g/3½ oz/½ cup	rice
100g/3½ oz/½ cup	red lentils, washed
250ml/9fl oz/1 cup	boiling water
2 tbsp	butter or margarine
1	large onion, chopped
8	medium tomatoes
1 tbsp	chopped mint
	salt and pepper
2 tbsp	oil
1 clove	garlic, crushed

1) Put the rice, lentils and boiling water in a pan and cover. Cook for 10 minutes.
2) Meanwhile, melt the butter or margarine and slowly fry the onion until deep golden.
3) While that is frying, slice the tops off the tomatoes and reserve. Scoop out the middles and chop.
4) Add the rice and lentils to the onion and mix well. Stir through the mint and season generously with salt and pepper.
5) Fill the tomatoes and replace the tops. Stand in a baking dish.

6) Mix the oil and garlic with the chopped tomatoes and pour around the stuffed tomatoes. Bake in a hot oven at 230°C/450°F/Gas Mark 8 for 10–15 minutes. Serve.

Dügün Pilavı

As we sat in Dalyan's most overpriced restaurant, a car drew up and out stepped a pair of young newlyweds. He was soberly suited, she wore an elaborate long white satin dress and veil. A different chair had to be fetched to accommodate its billowing folds. Their taxi driver sat with them as they all sipped Cokes. Why weren't they tucking into this Wedding Rice, or supping Wedding Soup (see page 4)? (Although I can imagine why they eschewed the 'mushed bull's balls' that the waiter so leeringly described!)

500ml/18fl oz/2 cups	vegetable stock
200g/7oz/1 cup	long grain rice
175g/6oz/1 cup	canned chick peas (garbanzos)
2 tbsp	butter or margarine, melted
	salt and pepper

1) Bring the stock to the boil, then add the rice and chick peas (garbanzos). Cook until the rice is tender and the liquid has been absorbed.
2) Pour over the butter or margarine and season well. Fluff up with a fork and serve.

Fırında Makarna

Extraordinary how the very ordinary is found in similar guises from one end of the globe to the other. This is a version of the nursery favourite, Macaroni Cheese. Baked in a dish, it is turned out and cut in wedges like a pie or cake as were some Victorian versions.

250g/8oz/1½ cups	2-minute cook macaroni
	boiling water
125g/4oz/½ cup	butter
1½ tbsp	plain flour
500ml/18fl oz/2 cups	milk
	salt and pepper
2	egg yolks
90g/3oz/¾ cup	Cheddar or Gouda cheese, grated

1) Cook the macaroni in the boiling water for 2 minutes. Drain and stir in half the butter.
2) Melt the rest of the butter and add the flour. Cook, stirring for 5 minutes, then gradually stir in the milk. Season. Take off the heat and beat in the egg yolks.
3) Pour half the sauce over the macaroni. Mix well and place in a greased baking dish.
4) Pour on the remaining sauce, cover with cheese and bake for about 20 minutes at 180°C/350°F/Gas Mark 4 until set and golden. Turn out and serve.
5) Most Turks, to my daughter's great delight, eat this with tomato ketchup (catsup).

İçli Köfte

These crunchy, chewy köfte are made with bulgar wheat. They are lightly spiced and enclose a centre of pine kernels and currants. Traditionally they were boiled but most restaurants now serve them deep-fried. You can roast them in a hot oven – just make sure that the oil in the roasting tin is preheated before you put in the köfte.

350g/12oz/2 cups	bulgar wheat
250ml/9fl oz/1 cup	boiling water
1 tsp	cumin
½ tsp	chilli powder
	oil
125g/4oz/1 cup	mushrooms, roughly broken up
125g/4oz/1 cup	shallots, chopped
4 tbsp	pine kernels
4 tbsp	currants
1 tsp	cinnamon

1) Put the bulgar, boiling water, cumin and chilli in a food processor and run on low speed for 5 minutes. Stop occasionally to scrape the mixture down from the sides.

2) Meanwhile, in a little oil, quickly fry the mushrooms and all but a tablespoon of the shallots. Add to the processor and whizz again for a couple of minutes.

3) Fry the remaining shallot with the pine kernels and currants. Take off the heat as the pine kernels begin to colour and add the cinnamon.

4) Divide the bulgar mixture into 8 patties. Place a pinch of the pine kernels on top of each. Laying the patty in the middle of your dampened hand, fold the sides around the pine kernel filling to enclose it. Gently roll it around to seal and form an egg shape.

5) Carefully lay them in a frying basket and lower into hot deep fat. Cook until nicely brown. Drain and serve.

Kuskus Pilavı

Couscous, so beloved of North Africans, is also a staple in Turkey. You can find it ready-cooked and frozen in some enterprising stores. This cheat's failsafe method, almost as fast, is not labour-intensive like the traditional way of damping, steaming, buttering and more steaming.

We prefer couscous to bulgar, its texture is lighter and less chewy. It is more refined so is not as nutritious as bulgar but, like pasta, it is a good starchy carbohydrate. You can, of course, add bits of vegetable, spices, nuts and raisins to the couscous but try it plain first!

250g/9oz/1½ cups	instant couscous – precooked, medium grade
1–2 tbsp	butter or margarine
1 tsp	salt
375ml/15fl oz/1½ cups	boiling water

1) Spread the couscous out in the base of a large flat dish. Dot with the butter and sprinkle over the salt.
2) Pour over the boiling water and cover tightly with foil or buttered baking paper. Bake at 180°C/350°F/Gas Mark 4 for 5 minutes. Fork up and serve.

İstanbul Pilavı

Leftover cooked, tinned or microwaved rice will cut preparation time in half.

200g/7oz/1 cup	long grain rice
	boiling water
	salt
75g/2½ oz/⅓ cup	butter or margarine
1	shallot, finely chopped
125g/4oz/1 cup	oyster mushrooms, cut into strips
90g/3oz/½ cup	peas, canned or frozen
pinch	saffron, soaked in 1 tbsp boiling water
50g/2oz/½ cup	slivered almonds
375ml/13fl oz/1½ cups	vegetable stock or water
50g/2oz/⅓ cup	firm smooth vegetable pâté – e.g. Tartex (optional)
50g/2oz/⅓ cup	pistachios

1) Cook the rice for 10 minutes in boiling salted water, then drain.
2) Melt the butter or margarine. Fry the shallot and oyster mushrooms quickly. Add the peas, saffron, almonds, stock and rice. Cook, stirring occasionally, until the liquid has been absorbed.
3) Cube the pâté if using and stir through the rice. Sprinkle with the pistachios and serve.

Eggs

Çilbir

Poached eggs in a yoghurt sauce. If you haven't time to do the paprika and butter, I have often seen its place taken by a dribble of tomato ketchup (catsup) or even chilli sauce.

4	large eggs
a knob	butter (to grease poacher cups)
	or
1 tbsp	vinegar
500g/1lb 2oz/2 cups	plain yoghurt
1 tsp	salt
1 tsp	paprika
1 tbsp	melted butter

1) Poach the eggs in an egg poacher or drop them into boiling water to which you have added the vinegar.
2) Beat together the yoghurt and salt. When set, drain the eggs and spoon over the yoghurt.
3) Mix together the paprika and butter and dribble on top of the yoghurt. Serve.

Fırında Yumurta

Baked, stuffed eggs.

8	large eggs, hard-boiled and peeled
1 large slice	white bread
a small bunch	spring onions (scallions), roughly chopped
2	bottled sun-dried tomatoes, drained and roughly chopped
2	egg yolks
	salt and pepper
1–2 tbsp	butter or margarine, melted

1) Halve the eggs and place the centres in a food processor with the bread, spring onions (scallions), sun-dried tomatoes and raw egg yolks.
2) Process in bursts to make a paste. Season with salt and pepper. Fill the egg whites with the paste.
3) Place on a baking sheet or dish. Drizzle with the butter or margarine and bake at 180°C/350°F/Gas Mark 4 for 15 minutes.

Ispanakli Yumurta

This is very similar to Eggs Florentine – fresh spinach wins every time in my book especially as you can buy it ready-washed in bags for speed. However, if needs must, you can at a pinch use drained canned or frozen spinach. Chard is also very good but needs a little longer cooking time.

50g/2oz/¼ cup	butter or margarine – you can use a bit less if you prefer
1 clove	garlic, crushed
1	shallot, finely chopped
500g/1lb/8 cups	ready-washed spinach – this seems a large amount but it cooks down very fast
4	large eggs
	paprika
	salt and pepper

1) Melt the butter or margarine and fry the garlic and shallot until yellowing.
2) Add the spinach, turning it about as if dressing a salad. Cook with a chopping/stirring motion, using a wooden spoon, until a soft thick purée is formed – about 7–10 minutes.
3) Make 4 depressions in the spinach, with the back of the spoon, and crack in the eggs. Dust each with paprika, salt and pepper.
4) Cover and cook over a low heat until the eggs are set – about 4 minutes. Serve.

Cook's Note

The spinach purée can be made in advance and spooned into the bottom of individual ramekin dishes. When needed, crack an egg over each and bake for about 10 minutes in a moderate oven, until set.

Mantarli Krep

Atatürk imported many French words into the Turkish lexicon, they just look a little different. A Turkish krep or crêpe is an eggy pancake or a more substantial omelette, depending on how you look at it. We came across it in the *tren Istasyon* (train station) restaurant at Adana. Use any filling you like from white cheese, parsley and garlic to spinach or cauliflower.

	oil for frying
1	red onion, diced
125g/4oz/1 cup	mushrooms, quartered
400g/14oz can	chopped tomatoes
1 tbsp	chopped parsley
300ml/11fl oz/1¼ cups	milk
4	eggs
115g/4oz/¾ cup	plain flour
pinch	salt

1) Heat a little oil in a pan and briefly fry the onion and mushrooms. Add the tomatoes and simmer for 10 minutes. Stir in the parsley and season.
2) Place the remaining ingredients in a blender or food processor and whizz on high speed to make a smooth batter.
3) Heat a little oil in a large frying pan. Pour in a quarter of the batter and swirl it around to evenly cover the base of the frying pan. Loosen the edges and flip over when the underside is golden and the top has set. Fry until lightly browned on the second side.

4) Slide onto a warm plate and place a quarter of the mushroom mixture on half of the krep. Fold over and serve. Repeat with the rest of the batter.

Mantar Yumurta

Mushrooms here take the place of the traditional minced beef or lamb.

1	medium onion, quartered
1 clove	garlic, peeled and halved
225g/8oz/2 cups	mushrooms, roughly broken up
1 tbsp	olive oil
a knob	butter or margarine
a pinch	ground coriander
	salt and pepper
2	tomatoes, diced
2 tbsp	chopped parsley
4	large eggs, beaten
4 tbsp	finely grated Parmesan
2 tsp	plain flour

1) Place the onion, garlic, mushrooms and oil in a food processor and using the pulse button, chop (mince) them quite finely.
2) Melt the butter or margarine and scrape in the mushrooms. Fry briskly until colouring. Add the coriander, salt and pepper.
3) Stir in the tomatoes and parsley. When the mixture is piping hot again, mix together the eggs, Parmesan and flour. Pour onto the mushroom mixture. Cover and cook until set – about 5 minutes. Serve.

Menemen I

A Turkish version of scrambled eggs, this dish is served both hot and cold. I found it in two distinctly different versions and as both were tasty, both recipes are included.

1 tbsp	butter
4	medium tomatoes, diced
1	large red (bell) pepper, diced
1	large yellow (bell) pepper, diced
4	large eggs, beaten
	salt and pepper

1) Melt the butter and fry the tomatoes and (bell) peppers until softened.
2) Season then stir in the eggs. Continue stirring over a low heat until the eggs are just set. Serve.

Menemen II

You can make this version of Menemen in individual ramekins.
Serve with crusty bread and a fresh green salad.

1 tbsp	olive oil
4	medium tomatoes, sliced
1	large red (bell) pepper, sliced
1	large yellow (bell) pepper, sliced
1	small green (bell) pepper, sliced
4	large eggs, beaten
	salt and pepper

1) Put the oil, tomatoes and (bell) peppers in a roasting tin in a
   hot oven – 220°C/425°F/Gas Mark 7 – for 10 minutes, until
   softened.
2) Make 4 depressions in the peppers with the back of a spoon
   and pour in the seasoned eggs. Return to the oven and bake
   until set, about 7 minutes. Serve hot or cold.

Soğanli Yumurta

Use sweet onions for this dish, either red, yellow, Spanish or shallots. Leeks can also be used.

1 tbsp	butter or margarine
300g/10oz/2 cups	onions, chopped
1 tbsp	plain flour
200ml/7fl oz/¾ cup	vegetable stock
1 tbsp	mushroom soy sauce or mushroom ketchup
4	eggs

1) Melt the butter or margarine. Fry the onion until colouring.
2) Stir in the flour. Cook for 1 minute, stir in the stock and mushroom soy sauce or mushroom ketchup.
3) When barely simmering, break the eggs onto the surface. Cover and cook until set – about 4 minutes. Serve.

Peynirili Yumurta

Eggs with cheese, this is almost fondue – serve with lots of bread as it is quite rich.

1 tbsp	butter
125g/4½ oz/1 cup	finely grated cheese, Cheddar or the Jewish Kashkavale
250ml/9fl oz/1 cup	good vegetable stock
4	eggs, beaten

1) Melt the butter, stir in the cheese.
2) Stir in the stock and then the eggs. Keep stirring until the eggs are set, serve immediately.

Tatlilar (Puddings)

Ay Çöreği

These melt-in-the mouth walnut turnovers are made in a crescent-shape, a potent national symbol in Turkey. This quick version uses ready-made, ready-rolled sweet flan pastry. It is found in the freezer or chill sections of bigger supermarkets. It is sometimes labelled 'pâté sucré'. If you cannot find it, you can of course make your own but this would take longer than 30 minutes as the dough would have to be chilled and rested.

300g/10oz	flan pastry (see above)
200g/7oz/nearly 2 cups	finely grated walnuts
90g/3oz/²/₃ cup	icing (confectioner's) sugar
2 tbsp	clotted cream (or use whipped cream)
75g/2¹/₂ oz/¹/₂ cup	small raisins (i.e. not Lexias)
1	egg, separated
¹/₂ tsp	ground cinnamon
¹/₂ tsp	water

1) If necessary, roll the pastry to 0.5cm/¹/₄ inch thickness – some ready rolled pastry is a little thicker than this.
2) Stamp out 7.5cm/3 inch rounds, re-rolling the trimmings.
3) Mix the walnuts, icing (confectioner's) sugar, cream, raisins, egg white and cinnamon. Put a spoonful on each pastry round. Beat the egg yolk with the water. Fold the pastry circles in half to form crescents, sealing with the egg yolk mixture.
4) Place on a baking (cookie) sheet lined with baking paper, brush with the remaining egg and bake for 15 minutes at 200°C/400°F/Gas Mark 6.

Ayva

Turkish or Greek shops are probably your best bet when looking for quinces. My tree produced only a very few every year until last year, when I had such a glut I made quince cheese and jelly. This year there is not a single one and I shall miss the sweetly fragrant smell of them cooking.

Look for them in the autumn – golden, slightly fuzzy and when ripe, exquisitely perfumed. Who needs air freshener – sit a quince in your fruit bowl!

3–4	large quinces, quartered, cored and thinly sliced
125ml/4½ fl oz/½ cup	boiling water
100g/3½ oz/½ cup	caster sugar
1	cinnamon stick, broken into 4 pieces
	kaymak (Turkish clotted cream), ice cream or yoghurt to serve

1) Lay the quince slices out in an ovenproof dish.
2) Pour the boiling water onto the sugar and stir until dissolved. Pour over the quinces.
3) Scatter on the cinnamon and cover.
4) Bake at 190°C/375°F/Gas Mark 5 for 20 minutes. Serve hot, warm or cold.

Cook's Note
Under-ripe pears can also be baked in this way. Add a few cardamom pods instead of the cinnamon.

Baklava

Sticky and sweet, baklava can be found in Greece and the Middle East, as well as in Turkey. This is not only a cheat's version but it is also by comparison a tiny tray full. In the windows of the *pastane* salvers of baklava, more than a metre/yard across, glisten under their syrupy glaze.

4 sheets	filo pastry, cut in half
4–5 tbsp	butter or margarine, melted
100g/3½oz/1⅓ cup	ground walnuts, hazelnuts or pistachios
4–5 tbsp	honey
1 tsp	orange flower water
1 tbsp	boiling water

1) Lay 1 sheet of filo into the base of an oblong cake tin, ensuring it fits well. Brush with the butter or margarine and sprinkle with the ground nuts. Repeat until you have used all 8 of the half sheets of filo.
2) Using a very sharp knife, cut the pastry from top to bottom, in strips 2cm/1 inch wide. Turn the tin through 45° and cut into strips of 4cm/1¾ inches wide, giving the traditional parallelogram shape.
3) Bake at 200°C/400°F/Gas Mark 6 for 20 minutes.
4) Just before the baklava has finished baking, mix together the remaining ingredients. When you take the baklava from the oven, pour the honey mixture all over it and ideally leave it to cool. It can be eaten hot if desired.

Balli Muz

Down around Alanya, on Turkey's Mediterranean coast, there are fields and fields of bananas, tumbling down the hillside alongside the spectacular coastal Highway 400. However, when we tried to buy Turkish bananas in Kizkalesi, further east, all we found were Ecuadoran ones (good bananas but...).

The other main ingredient in this dish is honey. Hives are found all over the forests and fields. Most villages have co-operatives to sell the honey. I made this pudding with a delicious pine honey from around Lake Köycegiz.

4	bananas, peeled and sliced
2 tbsp	butter (butter is better here for flavour reasons but you can use margarine)
4 tbsp	honey
4 tbsp	chopped pistachios

1) Fry the bananas in the butter for 1 minute. Add the honey, turning about carefully to avoid mushing the bananas. Allow to bubble hard for 1 minute – but be careful not to scorch the bananas.

2) Spoon into 4 small dishes and top with the pistachios. Serve warm or cold, with or without cream, yoghurt or ice cream.

Cook's Note
Other fruit, notably peaches, apricots, nectarines and pineapples can be treated this way. Some cooks add desiccated coconut, pine kernels and/or raisins. Let your fancy be your guide.

Firin Sütlaç

This is a baked rice pudding, with a glazed top. You need some
leftover cooked rice – if you have none, preparation time will
take a little longer.

750ml/1 pint 7fl oz/3 cups	full cream milk
175g/6oz/a scant cup	sugar
125g/4oz/²/₃ cup	cooked rice
1	egg yolk
1 tbsp	rice flour

1) In a saucepan, simmer the milk, sugar and rice for 10 minutes.
   Mix a little of the hot milk with the egg yolk and set aside.
2) Mix the rice flour with the water and whisk into the hot milk.
   Cook, stirring, for 3 minutes. Spoon into ovenproof dishes,
   top with the egg yolk mixture and bake at 190°C/375°F/Gas
   Mark 5 until nicely browned – about 15 minutes. Serve hot or
   allow to cool and chill well.

Kadayif Cevizli

This is the shredded wheat pastry again, this time soaked in syrup with walnuts.

You can add shelled pistachios as well as or instead of the walnuts.

As you serve only tiny pieces this quantity makes enough for at least 12 people, so don't panic at the amount of sugar!

This is best left to get quite cold before serving but you can eat it warm – serve it with cream or yoghurt to cut the sweetness.

450g/1lb/approx. 2–3 cups	kadayif pastry (cup quantity used depends on how compressed it is)
125g/4oz/½ cup	melted butter
225g/8oz/2 cups	roughly chopped walnuts
1 tbsp	ground cinnamon
450g/1lb/2¼ cups	sugar
500ml/18fl oz/2 cups	water
1 tbsp	lemon juice

1) Spread half of the kadayif in the base of a greased 25cm/ 10 inch square pan. Pour over half the butter. Sprinkle with the nuts and cinnamon, cover with the remaining pastry and drizzle over the rest of the butter.
2) Bake at 190°C/375°F/Gas Mark 5 for 20 minutes.
3) Meanwhile, boil together the sugar and water until syrupy. Add the lemon juice. Pour over the baked kadayif. Cool and serve.

Kaymaklı Kuru Kayısı

These luscious cream filled apricots are quick to make if you buy the 'ready to eat' dried apricots. These require no prior soaking and only a swift poaching in syrup. They are already stoned and split, so are easy to stuff. If unavailable, you just have to remember to pour some boiling water on the apricots earlier on in the day.

Kaymak, Turkish clotted cream, is hard to find. Greek yoghurt with added cream, creamy fromage frais, crème fraîche in a jar, or even a light cream cheese are all acceptable substitutes.

125ml/4½ fl oz/½ cup	water
150g/5oz/¾ cup	sugar
1 tbsp	lemon juice
250g/9oz/1½ cups	dried apricots (see above)
200g/7oz/1 cup	kaymak, yoghurt, fromage frais, crème fraîche or cream cheese
1 tbsp	ground hazelnuts

1) Bring the water and sugar to the boil. Add the lemon juice and apricots. Cover and cook for 5 minutes.
2) Using a slotted spoon, remove the apricots and spread them out in a cool place. Reduce the syrup until it is fairly thick.
3) When the apricots are cool, place the kaymak (or substitute) into a forcing bag and squeeze a little in the middle of each apricot. Place the filled apricots in a dish and dribble over the syrup. Sprinkle with the nuts and serve.

Kazandibi

This is a caramelized ground rice pudding. I have come across a very similar Russian dessert, using ground semolina in place of the rice. Watch it carefully under the grill (broiler) – caramelized is what you want with a lovely rich flavour, not burnt with that bitter back taste.

Kazandibi actually means 'bottom of the pot' (i.e. scorched) and is the name also given to the residue of Tavukgögsü, a pudding not included in this book as it consists of much boiled and pounded chicken breast.

60g/2oz/⅓ cup	ground rice
125g/4oz/½ cup + 1 tbsp	sugar
500ml/18fl oz/2 cups	milk
1 tbsp	butter or margarine
2 tbsp	icing (confectioner's) sugar
1 tbsp	rosewater

1) Whisk together the ground rice, sugar and milk in a pan. Stirring with a wooden spoon, cook over a moderate heat until quite thick.
2) Butter a heatproof baking dish and spread out the rice mixture. Dust thickly with the icing (confectioner's) sugar.
3) Place under a preheated grill (broiler) until the top is a rich brown. Cool and serve cut into squares with the rosewater dribbled over.
4) If left to go quite cold, the traditional way to serve it is to roll the edges under, with the caramelized top uppermost, so it

looks rather like a roulade at first glance – this is a bit fiddly and not for 30 minute cooks.

Cook's Note
The Russian version was served with a warm fruit compote – try a Kompostosu (see pages 118 and 122).

Keşkül

Another milky pudding that is traditionally eaten cold but can be eaten warm. Although almonds are specified, ground hazelnuts can be used instead and some cooks add coconut (this is not to my taste).

500ml/18fl oz/2 cups	milk
100g/3½oz/1¼ cup	ground almonds
50g/2oz/⅓ cup	ground rice
150g/5oz/¾ cup	sugar
4	cherries – glacé or fresh
a few	slivered almonds

1) Combine the milk, ground almonds, ground rice and sugar in a pan with a whisk. Slowly bring to the boil, stirring often. Then stir continuously, when simmering, until the mixture coats the back of a spoon.
2) Pour into four individual dishes and top each with a cherry and the slivered almonds. Serve hot or chill well and serve later.

Kiraz Kompostosu

There are two words in Turkish for cherry: Vişne is the sour cherry and Kiraz are the huge, dark, sweet cherries, more flavourful than any I have ever tasted. A kilo in a paper bag disappeared so fast we had to go back for more before we were half way up the street.

Don't bother to stone the cherries – you'll be there for hours, tell everyone it adds to the flavour. Anyhow, there'd be no 'Tinker, tailor, soldier, sailor…' This compôte is fabulous served warm with ice cream or thick yoghurt.

450g/1lb/a good 3 cups	big black cherries, without their stalks
90g/3oz/scant ½ cup	caster sugar
100ml/3½fl oz/⅓ cup + 1 tbsp	water
1	lemon

1) Put the cherries, sugar and water in a pan. Peel a strip of lemon zest about 5cm/2 inches long, making sure there is no pith. Add to the cherries and bring to the boil. Simmer for 10 minutes.
2) Add 1 tablespoon of lemon juice and cook for a further 2 minutes. Serve hot, warm or cold.

Kremalı Meyveler

This fruit salad is swirled through with cream and honey. Change the fruits according to what is in season. Anatolia has an unsurpassed fruit harvest, the flavours are full and rich, having ripened under the ever present summer sun and what a variety! Choose from apples and bananas to lemons and melons, or even mulberries and pomegranates: it is an endless list.

1	sugar or pineapple melon, cubed
3	figs, quartered
2	large ripe peaches, cubed
150g/5oz/1 cup	cherries
2 tbsp	honey (a clear pine, acacia or thyme honey is good)
1 tbsp	lemon juice
60ml/2fl oz/¼ cup	double (heavy) cream
2 tbsp	slivered almonds
2 tbsp	chopped pistachios

1) Mix the fruit together.
2) Combine the honey and lemon juice thoroughly. Slowly mix in the cream and stir through the fruit. Chill well.
3) Toast the almonds and pistachios lightly. Cool and sprinkle over the fruit before serving.

Revani

This grainy semolina cake can be served hot, warm or cold. It takes seconds to make so can be thrown together at the last minute. Maple syrup is a good substitute for the sugar syrup – in fact I prefer it. Honey, mixed with a little warm water can also be used.

100g/3½ oz/½ cup	semolina
60g/2oz/scant ½ cup	plain flour
2 tsp	baking powder
100g/3½oz/½ cup	sugar
3	eggs
115g/4oz/½ cup	soft butter or margarine
1 tsp	pure vanilla extract – much better than synthetic vanilla essence, read the label
250ml/9fl oz/1 cup	water
125g/4oz/⅔ cup	sugar
1 tsp	lemon juice
	yoghurt or kaymak (optional)
3	fresh figs, sliced (optional)
a pinch	ground cinnamon

1) Put the semolina, flour, baking powder, sugar, eggs, butter and vanilla in a food processor or mixer and beat until a smooth batter is formed – only 30 seconds or so.

2) Scrape the mixture into a greased 18cm/7 inch tin. Bake at 190°C/375°F/Gas Mark 5 for 20–25 minutes.

3) While the cake is baking, boil together the water and remaining sugar, simmering for 10 minutes. Add the lemon juice.

4) Turn the cake out, pour over the syrup and serve hot, warm or cold with a topping of yoghurt or kaymak, fresh figs and a dusting of cinnamon.

Şeftali Kompostosu

It is a sad fact of modern life that although we have more variety than ever in our supermarkets and stores, it is virtually impossible to find a ripe peach. This compôte solves the problem of what to do with those rock hard peaches that look so tempting and beautiful in their fuzzy-coated way but are inedible. If you are a perfectionist, scald and peel the peaches first – lesser mortals will enjoy the rosy blush the skin adds to the syrup.

6 peaches, diced
90g/3oz/scant ½ cup caster (fine) sugar
75ml/2½ fl oz/⅓ cup water

1) Put the peaches, sugar and water in a pan. Bring to the boil and simmer for 10 minutes.
2) Pour into a dish and serve hot, warm or cold.

Cook's Note
You can use the same method for fresh apricots and nectarines.

Tulumba

This pudding is served by street vendors and restaurants alike. It is similar to churros, the Spanish favourite – it is choux pastry, fried and then soaked in syrup. One each was certainly enough for us. It will test your sweet tooth. If you like rum babas, try this.

For speedy and/or a less sickly confection, use maple syrup and serve with kaymak or yoghurt and a Kompostosu (see pages 118 and 122). This may not be strictly authentic but it is good. Alternatively, if you want to be correct about it, serve tiny cups of strong unsweetened kahve and glasses of water.

Sometimes the paste is shaped into rings, sometimes it rejoices under the name Vezir's Fingers (what a creepy picture that conjures of an Ottaman potentate's sycophantic official with his fingers in every pie or pot of syrup!).

375ml/13½ fl oz/1½ cups	water
375g/13½ oz/scant 2 cups	sugar
1 tbsp	lemon juice
60g/2oz/¼ cup	butter or margarine
125g/4½ oz/1 cup	plain flour
2	eggs, beaten
	oil for deep frying

1) Put 250ml/9fl oz/1 cup of the water into a heavy based pan and add the sugar and lemon juice. Bring to the boil and simmer for 10 minutes.
2) Meanwhile, put the rest of the water in a nonstick pan with the butter or margarine. Heat until the fat melts. Tip in the

flour and cook, stirring until a soft ball leaves the sides of the pan cleanly. Tip into a mixer's bowl. Gradually beat in the eggs on a high speed.

3) Heat the oil. Scrape the paste into a forcing bag and pipe 7.5cm/3 inch lengths into the hot oil. When crisp and brown, remove from the oil, drain briefly on kitchen paper, then put into the syrup. Repeat until all the dough is used up. Serve.

Un Helvası

'Un' means flour and this is a rather odd pudding made from flour, butter, milk and sugar. Eaten hot, it is a little like eating warm fudge. It requires constant attention for the first 10–15 minutes then you just leave it for another quarter of an hour. So, spend 15 minutes cooking the main course, leaving it to bubble away while you are cooking the helva and then eat the main course while the helva is cooling a little.

Please note – you have to use butter. Let's face it, this is not a *healthy eating* recipe, the flavour depends on butter so make it with butter or not at all! You won't want to indulge that often, just have it once in a blue moon. It is very rich, this is ample for 8 sane people – some find it moreish and would disagree. I would serve some fresh fruit, peaches or grapes, afterwards.

125g/4½ oz/1 cup   plain flour
100g/3½ oz/¾ cup (less 1 tbsp)   butter
200g/7oz/1 cup   sugar
500ml/18fl oz/2 cups.   milk
a few   almonds, pistachios or hazelnuts

1) Cook the flour and butter together over a moderate heat, stirring constantly until the flour has turned a lovely nutty brown – it smells wonderful.
2) At the same time, over a low heat, in a separate pan dissolve the sugar in the milk and keep hot.

3) While stirring, gradually add the milk to the flour – taking great care as it bubbles up. Beat well until smooth and leave to stand for 15 minutes in a warm place.
4) Serve hot, placing egg-shaped spoonfuls on a dish and topping each with a nut.

Un Kurbabiyesi

These little fat diamond shaped biscuits, quite similar to shortbread, are served with çay and kahve (see pages 136 and 138).

Non-stick baking paper is almost essential for speed but greased greaseproof paper can be substituted. Butter, as with shortbread, bakes a better biscuit but make sure it is soft.

Halve the quantities if you only want a few to go with after dinner coffee, as petit fours. The biscuits keep happily for a few days in an airtight tin but make sure they are quite cold before storing.

> 115g/4oz/½ cup   soft butter
> 90g/3oz/⅔ cup   icing (confectioner's) sugar + some for dusting
> 250g/9oz/1¾ cups   plain flour

1) Place all of the ingredients into a food processor. Run until a soft ball of dough is formed.
2) Divide the dough between 2 sheets of baking paper. Form each into a long thin sausage – it is not necessary to be too finicky here, just pat and squeeze, rock and roll – speed is all! Cut 2cm/1 inch pieces – oblique slices give the traditional diamond shape. Spread out on the baking paper and slide onto baking (cookie) sheets.
3) Bake for 20–23 minutes at 180°C/350°F/Gas Mark 4 until pale golden and slightly firm. Set on a plate and dust with icing sugar.

Vişne Ekmek

Colette, the French writer and gourmet, had a very similar recipe for this simple cherry pudding from her native Burgundy. Turkish cherries are huge and full of flavour. The closest equivalent would be the bottled Eastern European ones that occasionally turn up in the supermarket or at delicatessens. Buy several jars when you see them and keep them on standby in the cupboard.

Turkish bread is like fat French loaves, they too are stale by the end of the day. This is a great way of using up leftover loaves.

Kaymak is the Turkish version of clotted cream and is the speciality of Afyon. It is less fatty tasting than Devon-style clotted cream but is rarely available. You could also use a creamy fromage frais – the low fat ones are just not right!

8 thick slices stale white bread
1 jar or can cherries in syrup
150g/5oz/²/₃ cup clotted cream

1) Lay out the bread on a baking sheet and place in a hot oven – 200°C/400°F/Gas Mark 6 until lightly browned. The time varies but usually takes about 7–10 minutes.
2) In the meantime, heat the cherries and syrup.
3) Place two slices of bread in a soup plate. Spoon over some cherries and serve with a spoon of clotted cream.

Yoghurt Tatlısı

Eaten hot this is a bit like a sponge pudding. More properly it is eaten cold. A syrup is always poured over. To save time and add flavour I use bottled fruits in syrup. This is a heavy syrup, as in stem ginger, not like a canned fruit salad. Turkish or Greek shops have quite a range – one of the best is kumquats as the acidity of the fruit cuts the cloying sweetness.

You can cook the pudding in one large basin but it will take longer to bake. If you don't have any individual pudding basins, darioles or ramekins, old heatproof tea cups will do or, cut the time further and bake in deep muffin or popover pans (allow for 2 each).

250g/9oz/1¼ cups	yoghurt
2	eggs
250g/9oz/1¼ cups	sugar
250g/9oz/1¾ cups	plain flour
1 tsp	baking powder
1 jar	preserved fruit in syrup (see above)

1) Whisk together the yoghurt, eggs and sugar at a high speed until pale and light.
2) Sift the flour and baking powder over the egg mixture. Fold through. Spoon into four small greased pudding basins or moulds.
3) Bake at 180°C/350°F/Gas Mark 4 for 20 minutes, until firm to the touch.
4) Turn out and spoon over some of the fruit and syrup. Serve hot or leave to cool.

Zerde

The Rough Guide to Turkey roughly describes Zerde as 'saffron-laced jelly'. It is a rice pudding, not milky but deep yellow with saffron, that is set with arrowroot. It takes less than the allotted 30 minutes to make BUT it should be left to cool and set firm. You can spoon it warm, it is quite a pleasant nursery pudding, but traditionally it is well chilled.

As with other recipes that call for leftover rice, use canned, microwaveable or quick-cook for speed if you haven't any.

Warning: Inferior saffron is not an economy – you will get neither the colour nor the flavour – you'll end up with a rather unattractive sludge. You have been warned!

175g/6oz/1 cup	cooked rice
750ml/25fl oz/3 cups	boiling water
150g/5oz/³/₄ cup	sugar
50g/2oz/¹/₃ cup	raisins
a good pinch	saffron
3 tbsp	arrowroot – cornflour (cornstarch) can be used but the clarity of the colour and the texture both suffer a little
50g/2oz/¹/₃ cup	pine kernels
1	pomegranate (optional)

1) Put the rice, 600ml/1 pint/2¹/₂ cups of water, sugar and raisins into a pan and simmer for 15 minutes. Meanwhile, soak the saffron in the remaining water.

2) Gradually combine the saffron water and the arrowroot. Then stir into the rice. Cook while stirring until the mixture thickens. Pour into individual bowls and leave to set. Top with pine kernels and pomegranate seeds, if liked.

Cook's Note
Some cooks omit the raisins or put them on top in place of the pomegranate seeds.

Drinks

Ada Çayı

This is sage tea, also called Island Tea. It is popular too in Crete. Sage is said to have many therapeutic properties, particularly for the digestion, nervous system, headaches etc. Turkish sage is more pungent than that found in Britain and North America, with an almost lavender-like edge to it. However, home-grown sage does make a good tea and it is worth a try.

a handful fresh sage
or
2 tbsp dried sage
boiling water
a few lemon slices
honey or sugar to taste

1) Place the sage in a clean teapot.
2) Pour on the boiling water. Cover and leave to brew in a warm place or covered with a cosy for 10 minutes.
3) Strain into glasses, serve with a slice of lemon. Sweeten to taste if desired.

Ayran

A salted yoghurt drink, Ayran can be found everywhere in Turkey. Stalls have big, whirling dispensers, there are tetrapaks in shops and hawkers have big churns full. Best served well chilled, it is the perfect accompaniment to Lahmacun, the spicy pizza (see page 57).

500g/1lb 2oz/2 cups	plain yoghurt – sheep's milk yoghurt is often nicest
500ml/18fl oz/2 cups	cold water
½ –1 tsp	salt
	fresh mint (optional)

1) Whizz the yoghurt, water and salt in a liquidizer until well blended.
2) Pour into four tall glasses and garnish with the mint leaves (optional).

Çay

In Turkey everybody drinks it, at all hours of the day or night. Whether you are buying a ring, looking at a carpet or deciding whether to take a room for the night, the likelihood is that a young boy will have been despatched to bring you çay – small glasses of hot, sweet black tea. Turks grow their own tea along the Black Sea coast. They use a two-tiered teapot, rather similar to those old fashioned French ones. A double boiler will work just as well.

Çay is an acquired taste – if you habitually enjoy a British cuppa or a Southern iced tea, it may be a bit of a culture shock but persevere, you could come to love it as much as the Turks who have a Çay Bahçesi (tea garden) in virtually every town park.

water
4 tsp loose tea leaves
sugar

1) Fill the bottom of a double boiler with water. Place the tea leaves in the top of the double boiler with 1–2 teaspoons of sugar. Sprinkle with 1 teaspoon of water. Cover and bring to the boil.
2) Pour 500ml/18fl oz/2 cups of the boiling water from the base onto the tea leaves in the top. Re-cover and allow to brew for 6 minutes over the remaining water in the base.
3) Strain into tea glasses, adjusting the strength to taste with extra boiling water as required. Serve with sugar as necessary.

Cook's Note
Add more boiling water to the tea leaves for further glasses.

Elma Çayı

This is Apple Tea, the preferred drink of my 9-year-old on our Turkish trek but drunk by all ages in cafés. *The Rough Guide to Turkey* sniffily says that instant apple teas have been nowhere near an apple, being merely chemical cocktails – that may be true of some but there are pleasant real apple teas available in freeze-dried form. As with most things in packets – check the label first! I have tried using the traditional dried apple pieces. We ended up with sci-fi blobs growing out of the pan and colonizing the cooker. The ever-expanding apple mush tried to take over the kitchen, eventually giving up the tiniest amount of not very pleasant liquid. No wonder most Turks use the granules! As these are not currently widely available, the following is a good substitute.

1 tbsp	pure concentrated apple juice – the thick brown syrupy stuff
	boiling water
1 slice	lemon (optional)
	sugar to taste

1) Put the concentrate into a glass. Leave a spoon standing in the glass before pouring on the boiling water. (Without the spoon the glass will crack.)
2) Add the lemon and sugar if using, stir and serve.

Cook's Note
A cinnamon stick and cloves may not be authentic but they are very good additions.

Kahve

Turkish coffee is famous but most Turks expect you to drink instant coffee as many of them do. Tiny and potent, it picks you up like nothing else. If you enjoy an espresso, you should try one of these. If you are more a double latte or cappuccino person, you probably will find kahve a bit much.

Ideally you require a cezve, a little pot with a long handle – however as most of us don't possess such a thing your smallest saucepan will suffice. The coffee must be very finely ground, so fine that it is powdered. It is possible to ask a specialist shop to grind it this well or some manufacturers are selling vacuum-packed ready-ground coffee.

4 heaped tsp   coffee (see above)
2 tsp   sugar (for orta sekerli – medium sweet)
250ml/9fl oz/1 cup   cold water

1) Put everything in a small pan. Mix carefully on a low heat, stirring from time to time until foam starts to rise.
2) Divide the foam between 4 tiny cups and return the pan to the heat. Bring to the boil and then pour into the cups, filling to the brim.
3) Serve but do not stir – this is why the sugar goes in first. Leave the sludge in the bottom of the cups.

Meyva Suyu

Although a secular country by law, most Turks are Muslim. As alcohol is proscribed for the faithful, there is a good selection of soft drinks available, especially fruit juices – Meyva Suyu. Our first introduction to Visne, the sour cherry juice was on a 'dry' flight on a Turkish air line. The richness of the flavour and the colour makes it a good alternative for those unable to drink red wine. Sadly Sour Cherry juice is difficult to find so I suggest the following. You can do the same with the other Turkish favourites – peach and apricot (Şeftali and Kayısı).

a large can or jar Morello cherries, stoned – try to find those
packed in their own juice
cold water
caster sugar to taste

1) Whizz the cherries in a blender. Strain through a fine sieve into a jug. Taste and add a little water and sugar as necessary.

Nane Limon

Many Mediterranean people drink mint teas – the Turks like theirs heavily flavoured with lemon. Use a potato peeler to ensure that none of the bitter white pith is included, otherwise the tea will be spoiled.

750ml/27fl oz/3 cups	water
	the peel of 1 lemon
a handful	mint
	sugar

1) Bring the water to the boil. Throw in the lemon peel and mint. Boil for 1 minute. Turn off the heat and leave to stand for 2 minutes.
2) Strain into glasses and sweeten to taste.

Rakı

Cloudy, innocently milky in appearance, Rakı, Turkey's national drink is quite pokey. If you want an authentic Turkish evening and you can't find it, you will have to substitute Greek Ouzo or a French Pastis instead.

ice cubes
1 bottle Rakı
cold water
2 glasses per person

1) Put several ice cubes in 1 glass per person. Pour in 1 shot of rakı over the ice. Add a splash of water.
2) Pour a plain glass of water for each person. Take a sip of the rakı then a gulp of the water and nibble çerez (see page 144) or meze. Repeat as necessary until rakı is finished or you fall off your chairs – now you know why those Ottamans lounged around on big cushions close to the ground!

Extras

Çerez

These are nuts and seeds you nibble with drinks, normally beer or rakı. On all the seaside promenades you'll find jolly barrows and stalls, lit up with lights and mirrors, toasting the çerez, turning them around and around while that irresistible smell fills the air. It is normal practice to get the barman to fetch you some çerez from the vendors when you order your drink or to have brought your own to the table!

At home a dry, heavy based skillet or frying pan is all you need. Alternatively, you can spread them out in a heavy roasting tin in a hot oven. Watch them carefully and shake them often if you choose to do it this way. The traditional chick peas (garbanzos) are best bought ready-roasted in your local wholefood or ethnic store – just give them a brief toasting at the last minute to freshen them.

a combination of: shelled pumpkin seeds
sunflower seeds
pistachios
shelled almonds
shelled filberts or hazelnuts
salt (optional)

1) In a heavy pan, spread out a single layer of your seeds and nuts. Over a moderate heat, stir or shake the seeds and nuts until they are lightly browned. You must keep them on the move otherwise they will not toast evenly.

2) Tip onto a clean tea towel or kitchen paper to cool. Sprinkle with salt (optional), and serve.

Cook's Note
The Turks are also very keen on milky fresh almonds that they eat wet – barrows are full of shelled almonds on mounds of dripping ice. Other nibbles include various dried fruits, especially luscious apricots.

Gözleme

Otherwise known as 'guzzle me', these are crêpe-like flat breads, cooked on remarkable convex curved griddles. Like enormous upside-down woks, the griddles sit over either charcoal or, more usually these days, a bottled gas flame. Often you will find a group of three women, all sitting on the ground, making gözleme. One rolls the dough with a broom handle rolling pin on a low round table, another prepares the fillings and the third cooks the pancakes. In unison they produce gözleme at a phenomenal rate – this is very fast food. On your own in 30 minutes you can rustle up at least half a dozen.

However if you are short of time, it is possible to substitute Lebanese Lavash bread, which is similar and is available in packets at some delicatessens and supermarkets.

Use leftovers, chopped hard-boiled or scrambled eggs or whatever you fancy to fill your gözleme.

285g/10oz/2 cups	strong plain flour – can be white or wheatmeal
1	egg
125ml/4½ fl oz/½ cup	milk
	oil

SUGGESTED FILLINGS	crumbled white cheese and parsley
	Humus (see pages 23 and 24)
	Manca (see page 31)
	honey
	Balli Muz (see page 111)

1) Put all of the dough ingredients except the oil into a food processor with a dough attachment. Run until a smooth, soft ball is formed. If it is very sticky add a little extra flour.
2) Pinch off a piece of dough the size of a walnut and, on a lightly floured surface, roll out as thin as possible.
3) Brush lightly with the oil. Fold over, brush and fold again. Roll out very thinly.
4) Place on a preheated griddle and cook on both sides until speckled. While one gözleme is cooking, roll the next.
5) When cooked and still warm, roll or fold around your chosen filling.

Cook's Note
The dough can be prepared several hours in advance and left, covered, in a cool place, until needed.

Kahvalti

The pleasures of bed and breakfasting in Turkey's *pansyions* and small hotels are many – kahvalti (breakfast) on the roof or terrace is certainly one of them. In the larger establishments this delightful feast has suffered from portion control, prepackaging and serious meanness. Family-run places are, on the whole, generous and thoughtful. From the home-made cherry preserves of the Nil Motel and the still warm bread of the Panorama Pansyion to the endless glasses of çay, are made memories of what breakfast can be, instead of the usual hectic rush. Try this on a lazy Sunday morning. If you can, eat outside in the sunshine. Otherwise, turn up the heating, throw on a bright blue cloth, have yellow daisies – put some colour into the morning!

4	freshly hard-boiled eggs
	black olives
4	tomatoes, sliced
1	small cucumber, sliced
5 slices	watermelon, sliced in triangles
200g/7oz/1 cup	fresh white cheese, cut in thick slices
	fresh crusty bread
	unsalted butter
	honey and/or good jam – preferably cherry
	or strawberry, with big bits of fruit in
	lots of çay (see page 136)

1) Lay everything out on the table and tuck in.
P.S. You can take much longer than 30 minutes to EAT it!

Peynirli Pide

Turkey's equivalent of the pizza parlour is the *pide salonu*. In the centre of Fethiye, it was a pleasure just to sit and watch the dexterity of a young man from Antalya who cherishes a dream of one day opening his own *pide salonu* in a British city.

This is a cheese pide – both the white cheese and the melting cheeses are used, so take your pick. If you crack an egg on each pide before baking it becomes a Yumurtali pide.

285g/10oz/2 cups	strong plain flour
1 heaped tbsp	dried instant yeast
½ tsp	salt
125ml/4fl oz/½ cup	warm water
200g/7oz/1 cup	white cheese, crumbled
	or
200g/7oz/1½ cups	Cheddar, grated
2 tbsp	parsley, chopped
	olive oil

1) In a food processor, knead the flour, yeast, salt and water until it is a soft, smooth dough. Leave it in the processor bowl until 10 minutes before you need it.
2) Divide into 4 and roll each out thinly to a long flat strip, 7.5cm/ 3 inches wide. Place on a baking sheet. Cover the middle of the strip with cheese and sprinkle with parsley. Fold the edges up and over to give a 1cm/½ inch border all the way around.
3) Bake in the hottest possible oven until puffed and lightly browned. Drizzle with a little oil. Serve cut in pieces.

Pide

Looking down from the balcony we had a bird's eye view of the tables below. Whatever anyone ordered, whether a simple bowl of Mercimek Çorbası (lentil soup, see pages 6 and 7) or an enormously lavish spread of meze, a pide, fresh from the oven would always be brought. Pide is a long, slightly puffed flat bread. Show-off chefs make them anything up to 1.10 metres/4 feet long. A domestic oven won't allow you such exhibitionist traits, you'll need to content yourself with more modest pide. However, you must crank your oven up as hot as it will go and you must use a really heavy duty baking sheet. I have a cast iron griddle that works fine and a friend uses preheated leftover terracotta floor tiles. This mimics the floor of the woodfired brick ovens normally used for cooking pide.

300g/10oz/2 cups	strong plain flour
1 heaped tbsp	dried instant yeast
½ tsp	salt
125ml/4fl oz/½ cup	warm water
	oil
1 tbsp	sesame seeds
1 tsp	black cumin seeds

1) In a food processor, knead the flour, yeast, salt and water until it is a soft smooth dough. Leave it in the processor bowl until 10 minutes before you need it.

2) Divide into 4 and roll each out thinly to a long flat strip, 5cm/2 inches wide. Place on a baking sheet. Brush lightly with oil and sprinkle with sesame and cumin seeds.

3) Bake in the hottest possible oven until puffed and lightly browned. Rush to the table.

Simit

First cousin to the Jewish bagel, simit are sold by street vendors and bakers all over Turkey. Like bagels, they are tight and chewy, and strangely moreish.

Young boys on the beach at Kizkalesi wandered up and down between the parasols with great turrets of simit on salvers balanced on their heads, the towers echoing the romantic Maiden's Castle in the sea behind them.

300g/10oz/2 cups	strong plain flour
1 tbsp	instant dried yeast
1 tbsp	butter
100ml/4fl oz/a scant ½ cup	warm water
	salt
	boiling water
1	egg yolk
1–2 tbsp	sesame seeds

1) Using the dough attachment, process the flour, yeast, butter, water and a large pinch of salt until a smooth ball is formed.
2) Divide the dough into 4. Roll each quarter into a long sausage – 25cm/10 inches long. Twist each sausage around into a ring. Poach each ring in the boiling salted water for half a minute.
3) Place them on a baking sheet. Brush with the egg yolk and sprinkle with the seeds. Bake for 20 minutes at 200°C/400°F/Gas Mark 6, until nicely browned.

Index